Lowell Sheppard lives in Japan with his wife and two sons, and is founder and director of Adventures in Purpose; Asia Director of HOPE International Development Agency; a fellow of the Royal Geographical Society; President of Japan Event Management and Bouken International Corporation and a motivational speaker. He has been active in the non profit sector for 30 years founding organizations such as Novimost and Whose Earth, and was director of British Youth for Christ. He is author of several books including *Boys Becoming Men* (Paternoster) and *Chasing the Cherry Blossom* (Lion). He has also been a contributor to various publications including *The Christian Herald* and *Japanzine*.

Never Too Late

Ten tips for changing the course of your life

LOWELL SHEPPARD

MONARCH
BOOKS

Oxford, UK & Grand Rapids, Michigan, USA

First published in the UK in 2005 by Monarch Books
(a publishing imprint of Lion Hudson plc),
Mayfield House, 256 Banbury Road, Oxford OX2 7DH
Tel: +44 (0) 1865 302750 Fax: +44 (0) 1865 302757
Email: monarch@lionhudson.com
www.lionhudson.com

Distributed by:
UK: Marston Book Services Ltd, PO Box 269,
Abingdon, Oxon OX14 4YN
USA: Kregel Publications, PO Box 2607,
Grand Rapids, Michigan 49501

ISBN-13: 978-1-85424-722-3 (UK)
ISBN-10: 1-85424-722-0 (UK)
ISBN-13: 978-0-8254-6101-9 (USA)
ISBN-10: 0-8254-6101-4 (USA)

British Library Cataloguing Data
A catalogue record for this book is available
from the British Library.

Book design and production for the publishers by Lion Hudson plc.
Printed in Great Britain.

Contents

In memory of GG

Dedicated to Ryan and Mackenzie

Prologue

**"The greatest danger for most of us
is not that our aim is too high and we miss it,
but that it is too low and we reach it."**

Michelangelo, artist of the 16th century

It came as a surprise.

Not being an American, I knew little of Benjamin Franklin. Other than the fact that he was a founding father of the United States and had once flown a kite with the express intention of attracting a lightning bolt, my knowledge of him was virtually nil. That changed on my fiftieth birthday.

The occasion was the opening ceremony of the US pavilion at the World EXPO in Nagoya, Japan. Three things impressed me that day: the pulsating performance of *taiko* drummers; the choice of a kite as the motif for the American treatment of the EXPO theme, Discovering Nature's Wisdom; and a hologram of Benjamin Franklin. Following an outdoor performance of the drummers, during which I gazed at the kite dangling above the stage, Franklin led us through the pavilion where we were rained on, struck by lightning, rumbled by thunder and impressed by his irrepressible curiosity and zest for life and living. I left the pavilion realizing how little I knew of this man, whose discovery of electricity and political innovations changed the world.

Historians have never been able to pigeonhole Franklin, whose restlessness did not make it easy for him to live a quiet and cosy life. The man was always on the move. The diversity of his life and the breadth of his accomplishments are impressive. His intellect and interests knew no inhibitions. He was not afraid of change and he regularly seized opportunities despite the risks. For him, it was never too late, nor too early, to explore new business ventures, literary projects, scientific inquiries, personal relationships or political concepts.

I left the US pavilion that cold March morning with more than a press packet: I had glimpsed a man's dream and had been stirred by Franklin's hunger to extract from life all that he could. Benjamin Franklin's passion for "more than the predictable" was nourished by his daring to live on the edge; he was always seeking to discover new things about his world and himself.

Never Too Late (NTL) advocates change. It is aimed at people who are restless, who harbour a gnawing dissatisfaction with the state of their lives. Those who fit this description are not few in number. It is such a common phenomenon, particularly for those in their forties, that the media have given it a name: midlife crisis. Usually spoken with a disparaging tone, the term is used to describe all kinds of behaviour, ranging from taking up new hobbies and buying expensive toys to making dramatic career changes or selling up everything and retreating to the hills of the south of France. This book seeks to look at midlife crisis through a different lens. Rather than suggesting it is something to be avoided, NTL advocates the notion that midlife crisis is in fact a divine alarm system aimed at awakening dormant dreams.

When I turned 40, the alarm, faint at first, was activated. In my thirties, I worked long hours, motivated by a subtle but strong belief that I was indispensable to the "cause". The result: I lost my health, nearly lost my wife and contracted a classic case of burn-out. I knew something had to change. But I felt trapped. We had two children and a mortgage, and I carried a deeply ingrained work ethic that caused me to feel guilty at the thought of letting colleagues down.

Applauded by some, criticized by others, I set my face towards re-evaluating my life and my dreams. The decision to go against the grain, take a break and put my wife's dreams ahead of my own brought changes – some dramatic, such as moving halfway around the world, others small and private. All the choices I made, big and small, involved risk. Ten years on, I can report that I have not only survived navigating through a minefield of changes, but as I enter my fifties, my body, my health, my marriage and my sensc of personal well-being have never been stronger.

It has not been a solo journey. I have always had people as mentors: some with deliberation, others without their knowledge. Over the last ten years the list of people who have made an imprint on my life has grown. A few of them have accompanied me on bike journeys, others have collaborated with me on various projects, while others still I have simply observed from a casual distance, inspired by their outlook, character and balance of life. My decision to move to another country was humbling, and I resigned myself to being a student again, learning from others. That decision alone changed my life. The tips for changing life's course found in this book are not new but are derived from ancient wisdom, passed down through the generations, with the intent of helping people experience what was once described by Jesus as "life to the full". Some of my mentors are older than me, while others are younger, but from each I have gleaned wisdom that has forever changed me.

You may ask: Is this more formulaic jargon: a book filled with over-hyped, motivational gibberish? I hope not! Yes, I do want you to be motivated, even inspired, but the book is rooted in real life, recognizing that things do not always go right. On its pages are practical strategies for keeping your dreams alive and celebrating every phase of life and the changes it brings. It builds, in part, from my research into adolescent development and the human need for adventure. NTL is for men and women who are not prepared to settle for the mundane. I suspect that some will refuse to read further than this prologue, either because they are content with their lives now, or because they are concerned that the book may provoke unsettling introspection. If you are of the first type, I congratulate you: you have found what you are looking for and are among the fortunate few. But if you fit the second description, I encourage you to draw on your inner courage and read on. That simple decision itself will result in untold dividends.

The tips in this book are neither new nor restricted to

one culture. They are rooted in age-old wisdom, and come from the four corners of the globe. But before I go on, let me take you to a London pub in Knightsbridge, where three friends are meeting. One of them is bringing extraordinary news.

The reunion, early January

Jud dashed down Brompton Road at breakneck speed, eager to share the news. He was still in a state of shock and did not know whether to laugh or cry. As he neared the entrance of the pub he slowed to gain his composure.

"Breathe deeply and show a bit of sobriety," he said to himself.

Standing outside looking in, he cast his mind back to that night two decades earlier when the group had formed. He and his friends were at a celebratory party on the night of their gradua-tion; united in drunken bliss, they had declared unwavering com-mitment to their dreams and pledged that they would not fall into the same trap as their parents who, in their view, had embraced the mundane and were ensnared in a life of drudgery, predictability and regret.

"The pact is forever," they had exclaimed as they formed what looked like a rugby scrum of seven men and five women.

They decided to have a reunion at this pub every five years, not only to hold each other to account, but also to inspire each other to chase their dreams, no matter what. They called them-selves the Dream Weavers. During the web-publishing boom years later, someone commented that they were fools for not having patented the name. They chose it because it aptly described their aspiration: to weave all that they would do into the pursuit of their dreams, leading integrated yet diverse lives, never settling for the status quo.

Their numbers had dwindled over the years, and as far as Jud knew, only two besides him would make it to this reunion. Most of the members had fallen away because of "busyness". A few saw each other from time to time, and email messages were occasionally circulated with pictures of babies, new houses or holiday snapshots: typically of the sender, standing on a beach holding a drink and sporting a grin. Jud seldom reciprocated but he did enjoy getting the news sent by others. He had not intended to attend this gathering, a decision confirmed by the untimely death of his father just ten days before. But the surprise package given to him by his father's lawyer immediately after the funeral changed his plans and not only made the trip to London possible, but also imperative.

Awakening

**"The best way to make your dreams
come true is to wake up!"**

Paul Valéry, French poet

**"Glorious it is when wandering
times have come."**

Inuit proverb

I was opposed to goal-setting. Once, when riding on a bus in northern Thailand, I debated the merits of the notion with a man twice my age. I have not seen him since, but I owe him, big time. The conversation stayed with me like an uncomfortable pebble in a shoe: I was always aware of it, always irritated by it, and always feeling I had to do something about it.

I came of age during the flower-power movement. At the time, I eschewed "goal-setting", believing it was more important to "be" than to "do". My policy of responding to opportunities rather than creating them took me to the refugee camps of Thailand. While I was there, I was asked to guide a well-known American broadcaster and his TV crew around Thailand. They were filming a documentary about the South East Asia refugee crisis.

One evening, while relaxing over a meal near the Cambodian border, the American asked me what my life's goals were. I recall feeling irritated by this intrusive query, and after pausing for a moment I told him proudly I had none. I explained that I felt it was God's will for me to drift from one opportunity to the next. It was not my business to tell God what I should do and where I should be. It was God's prerogative to tell me! I explained that I was content to drift rather than to dream.

It was a classic case of "double think". In part I believed what I was saying, but to state it required me to dismiss images that impregnated my imagination: images of myself as a married man, a father, crossing deserts and vast plains as feats of endurance, sailing boats, writing books, starting organizations and companies, changing the world, etc. These were dreams that had been with me since childhood. Somehow, in the process of growing up, the credibility of those dreams had become undermined by the notion that they were self-centred and that I was powerless to make them a reality.

I suppose part of my thinking was based on the false

notion that our lives are determined by forces outside of our control. "Whatever will be will be, the future's not ours to see, *que sera sera...*" had become my life's theme song. Dreams, I concluded, were to be ignored.

The man looked at me for a moment and, without responding, turned and looked out the window.

Eventually, as you would expect, my views changed. There was one particular turning point five years after the conversation in Thailand. I had since married and my work took us to North Yorkshire where we lived in a cottage on a farm. One evening, while sitting in front of the fire, I had an idea. I immediately made an instant and out-of-character decision to call a person I hardly knew, to see if he would be interested. The gentleman was positively enthusiastic and asked me to send him a written proposal and a plan for implementation. I hung up, feeling charged and gratified. The buzz that I experienced was out of proportion to the actual importance of the idea, but the simple decision to act brought unexpected pleasure. It was a small but significant turning point.

The proposition that dreams are good and they require us to get off our backsides and do something about them seems elementary and obvious. But some people live with a debilitating sense of fatalism that erodes the soul and prevents positive and constructive action. It is as if the engine is turned on, but left to idle. Yet all it takes is to put the car into gear, place the foot on the accelerator and get going. It is never too late to awaken the soul.

Some of you are about to put this book down, dismissing it as irrelevant or unrealistic. You believe that life is not always easy and fun, that it requires you to be responsible, stable and committed to family and colleagues. I agree! To lead a meaningful life, one must take on responsibilities that are not always pleasant or rewarding and that require lots of sweat, suffering and perseverance. But some people have such an extreme sense of responsibility that they develop an imbalance, a sort of disorder of the ego, which leads them to feel that projects would not survive without their involvement.

In my thirties, I was busy. I was overcommitted, overweight, seldom home for supper, and my health was suffering. My busyness was caused by an ego-driven belief that I was indispensable. It wasn't until I was forced off the treadmill for six weeks by illness that I realized that the organization I was responsible to lead was carrying on quite nicely without me. The sickness was a wake-up call and was followed by a period of reflection lasting nearly three years. The roots of my acute sense of responsibility went deep and it took some time for me to loosen the soil of my soul and free myself. I finally concluded that not only was my health at risk if I continued on the same path, but so was my marriage. The job itself was not the problem; it was my attitude towards it that needed reform. I needed to rediscover my passion and my dreams. I was uncertain what my dreams were or what they should be. So I had to borrow one: my wife's. Dreams propel, inspire and infect others, and I was drawn forward by hers. She opened up a new land and a new culture, and encouraged me to explore new opportunities. For her, the dream involved a homecoming: for me, well, I felt like I was moving to Mars. We actually moved to Japan.

The geographical, cultural and linguistic changes were dramatic, but other changes were gradual and incremental. Every decision that we made confirmed for me that life is full of options, and that we shape the future by our choices. Indecision, on the other hand, results in acceptance of a life by default. We are either pulled forward by our dreams or we drift. You have the power to choose whether to take charge of your life or succumb to external forces. It is never too late to set your compass on a new course, explore new worlds and delight in fresh discoveries. Whether you are seeking a new career or simply want to take up cycling at the weekends, this book is aimed at helping you take the necessary steps to achieve your goal responsibly and thoughtfully. It is designed not only to inspire and awaken dormant dreams, but also to provide clues to the mystery of personal re-invention. These tips, gleaned from others wiser than me, have helped me on my journey of change and I trust they will help you on yours.

The journey begins with a map; every traveller needs one. Maps not only help us know where we are going, but they also reveal secrets. These hidden truths make the process of getting to our destination a great adventure. So if you are ready, let's take the first step to embracing the future and realizing your dreams.

An unfinished Guinness

Jud could hardly contain his excitement as he entered the pub. It appeared much the same as it had on the night he and his friends had made their collective pledge. The sticky beer stains on the deep-pile rug, the imbedded odour of pipe and cigar wafting from the velvet drapes, and a string of customers leaning against the brass rail in front of the dark wood of the bar evoked memories of evenings of friendship and fine conversation. A large man and a tiny woman were serving drinks with an air of joviality. The ambience of the place calmed Jud more than his own words had just outside.

Robert and Sarah were already there, exchanging pleasantries and catching up on family and personal news. Jud had written to each of them the week before by email and told them that a sudden change of plans had made it possible for him to come to London and that he would tell them more when he arrived.

Jud had always felt challenged by Robert and Sarah. He admired them, but also felt uneasy around them. Of all the friends who formed Dream Weavers, Robert and Sarah were the ones who needed least to attend: they were living their dreams. All of them had completed their postgraduate work at the London School of Economics with a view to gaining employment with a large company, bank or financial institution. Sarah, though, within a week of the first Dream Weavers meeting, phoned each and every member of the group and said the formation of the group had made her realize that her passion was not economics but medicine. She announced that she had decided to return to university, but this time as a medical student. It took several more years of study before she finally became a general practitioner in the north of England. She seemed to love her life and her job.

Robert was a Canadian whom Jud had met at university; they graduated together and moved on to the LSE at the same time. He was among Jud's closest friends. Like Sarah, Robert soon decided that the corporate ladder was not for him. After only three years, he decided to move to Asia and set up his own business in one of the tiger economies there. His business was successful and although affected by the Asian currency crash of the mid-1990s, it survived. Jud was glad to see them.

"Hey!" Robert and Sarah said in unison.

"Hey!" Jud replied. "I have news for you, but let me buy a round of drinks first. The usual, I suppose?" A few moments later, he returned with three pints of Guinness and slid in beside Sarah on the velvet-covered bench.

"Whassup?" Robert asked.

Jud stared at his pint of dark ale, examining the gathering head. It provided him with a moment to gather his thoughts. He looked up and said, "My father just died."

"Oh, I'm so sorry!" Sarah exclaimed.

"No, I'm fine. In fact I'm great," Jud said, feeling embarrassed by the enthusiasm in his voice.

Sarah and Robert both looked perplexed. "But I thought your relationship with your father had improved," Sarah queried.

"Oh yes, you're quite right and it's been awful to have lost him. The cancer that took him was savage; it came so quickly... I know that death came as a relief for him."

"I can understand that death came as a relief to your father," said Robert, "but it doesn't explain that silly grin that's pasted on your face. You look like you just won the lottery."

Jud took a gulp of his Guinness as the two sat waiting for him to continue.

"Well, although I miss him terribly and I'm struggling to come to terms with everything, he left me a surprise."

Jud's relationship with his father had not always been a good one. Growing up, Jud rarely saw him because of the demands of work. When he did return home late from the office or after a long business trip, Jud's father seemed quiet and distant. He was a middle manager in a large company, with ambitions to rise to the top. It was evident to Jud at an early age that career aspirations governed the choices his father made and superseded his commitment to the family. That's not to say he wasn't responsible. He was faithful to Jud's mother and did his best to have at least a short conversation with Jud a few times a week. He always bought gifts for Jud and tried to be a good father. But deep down, Jud believed that his father's job was more important than he was.

This changed when Jud's mother died. Her death sparked a period of reflection and re-evaluation, and over time Jud and his father not only became friends but his father became Jud's role model. This development came as a surprise. Jud had never wanted to be like him, but gradually, over the last ten years, Jud's father began to represent everything Jud wanted to be.

"Get on with it, Jud. Tell us," Sarah said.

"Well, right after the funeral, the lawyer asked to see me. So I stepped outside and he presented me with a package. As you know, I'm the only child and as Mom died a few years ago I'm the sole heir. The lawyer told me what I'd expected to hear: except for a few shares and some land, my father didn't have much. But there was a surprise package. The lawyer told me to open it and inside there was a bundle of envelopes, each with a number. Ten of them had a number from 1–10 on them and the eleventh was blank. The lawyer told me to read the letter in the blank envelope and then he would be happy to answer any questions I had."

"The letter?" Sarah and Robert asked at once.

"Yep, a letter. I have it with me." Almost trembling, Jud took it out of his breast pocket, unfolding it slowly and deliberately. Then, after re-reading the first few lines again to himself as if to convince himself that he had got it right and that he was not dreaming, he read the letter aloud, eerily hearing his father's voice in his own.

Dear Jud,

You are reading this letter because I am gone. I do not have many material possessions to leave you but I do have some advice and experiences I want to share with you. In the last ten years, I have learned so much about what it means to live – really live – a large and meaningful life. Therefore, in addition to the few assets I must burden you with, I am bequeathing to you a "journey of discovery". In the bank account (details enclosed), you will find a sum of money that should pay for about ten to twelve weeks of travel. Kathryn (you can thank your wife for being an enthusiastic collaborator, visiting me in hospital and helping me write these letters) has told me that you have over three months of leave coming to you. So I know that taking the time is not a problem.

I am proud of you. You have worked hard and are advancing well in your company. I know you are busy, but I want you to do something for your old man; I want you to take the time coming to you and go on a journey. It is a journey I had wanted to make with you and I was saving up money to do so. But perhaps this is better ... a solo journey will help you internalize it and reflect on its insights and discoveries at a deeper level. I have met interesting and diverse people through the course of my life, particularly in the ten years since your mother died. I have learned a lot from them and been enriched by visiting the places where they live.

There isn't enough money to allow you to travel in the way you have become accustomed, staying in top-notch hotels and flying business class. It will be a challenge for you to make it around the world on the budget I have set. But believe me, the rewards will be great if you succeed, for along the way you will discover clues that will help unravel the mystery of how to live a large life.

One last thing: in the folder the lawyer gave you, there are ten envelopes. Open each of them in the correct order and at the designated destination. Each envelope will reveal where to go next. Your first stop is a place from which hundreds of adventurers have set out to explore the four corners of the world: the Royal Geographical Society in London. Do not open Envelope 1 until you are standing at its entrance.

With great love,
Your father

There were a few moments of silence when Jud finished reading. Sarah was the first to speak. "Well, what are we waiting for? Let's go."

"What? You haven't finished your Guinness," Jud said.

"C'mon, I can get another later – let's hurry. I've got a train to catch in three hours and I'm curious to know why your father has you starting at the Royal Geographical Society. Besides, I've never been there and this is a great excuse to go. We can see you off on your world tour from there."

Robert was already at the bar paying the bill while Sarah tugged at Jud's arm. He took one last gulp, grabbing his bag with the other hand as he was yanked from the table.

The three friends stepped briskly out of the pub and set off. They weren't entirely sure where the Royal Geographical Society was, but Sarah thought it was somewhere in the vicinity of the Royal Albert Hall across the road from Hyde Park.

1. Navigation

"The secret of getting ahead is getting started. The secret of getting started is breaking your complex, overwhelming tasks into small, manageable ones, and then starting on the first one."

Mark Twain, American author

"The day one starts out is not the time to begin one's preparations."

Nigerian proverb

"A journey of a thousand miles begins with one step."

Lao Tzu, ancient Chinese philosopher

Lost in London

Leaving Harrods to the right, the three friends crossed over Brompton Road and darted down a side street, searching for a route to Hyde Park. Becoming disoriented, they found their way back to Brompton Road and finally, they found a route that took them through the churchyard of Holy Trinity Brompton and a labyrinth of leafy residential streets, until they eventually arrived at Queen's Gate. What should have been a 15–20 minute walk had taken over an hour and they still hadn't arrived at the Royal Geographical Society. Sarah thought the Society faced Hyde Park somewhere between the Serpentine and Kensington Palace. To their right they could see the unmistakable dome of the Royal Albert Hall and guessed that their goal lay in the opposite direction. Rain was threatening but the sun was putting up a valiant struggle, occasionally scoring a small victory against the greyness of the day.

After a few minutes Kensington Palace came into view. Sarah commented that the last time she had been to this part of London was to lay flowers the week after Princess Diana died. Jud and Robert nodded in silent remembrance. The Royal Geographical Society was nowhere in sight, so they retraced their steps past Queen's Gate. Finally, they arrived at their destination just a few yards beyond the Royal Albert Hall. They stopped outside the main entrance and laughed at the length of time it had taken them to get there. But they had made it and gave each other a celebratory high five.

"Well, go ahead, do it!" Sarah commanded.

"Do what?" Jud asked.

"Open the envelope, you twit," she replied.

Robert and Sarah peered into Jud's bag as he pulled out the large package containing the ten envelopes, each with a number written on it. Jud rummaged for the envelope marked 1 and opened it, finding three items inside. The first was a card with his father's name and the word "fellow". It was his father's membership card.

The second item was a small, sealed envelope with a written instruction on it saying it should be opened and read when Jud had only 30 minutes left at the Society. The third item was a postcard:

Dear Jud,

Welcome to my favourite place in London: the Royal Geographical Society. As you walk through its corridors, be mindful that many great adventurers and explorers have done the same. People like David Livingstone, who discovered a goodly portion of Africa; Sir Edmund Hillary – he and Sherpa Tensing were the first two men to conquer the world's highest peak; and many more famous people. They found this place to contain treasures that inspired and offered practical guidance for those who dared to explore the unknown. Take some time to meander and make sure you allow plenty of time to explore the map room, where you will find the grandest and largest collection of maps in the world. Do not cut your time short. I only visited a couple of times, but on each occasion it fuelled my love of the world and my hunger for discovery.

Love, Dad

Tip 1: Get a map

I like maps. I have a personal collection but since it does not contain any precious or priceless cartographic documents, I suppose I am more a gatherer of maps than a collector. In our house I have a map room that also doubles as our dining room. I get a sense of space, history and travel each time I pass through, which is many times a day. In my office I have a container full of maps that I occasionally sort through, dreaming of places both far away and close by. Recently, I was sorting through this bulging bin and found myself reliving old adventures and dreaming of new ones as I rummaged through the hodgepodge of torn, well-travelled maps collected from various parts of the globe. They are important to me as I relive memories and plan the adventures that will create new ones.

In addition to hard-copy maps, I also have a Global Positioning System for my bicycle and a navigational system in my car. They both come in handy when negotiating the maze of streets in Japanese towns and cities. When the navigation system isn't working I feel a sense, not so much of lost-ness, but of loss itself: I miss its companionship.

There are three reasons I like maps:

1. I like to know where I am going.
2. I like to know where I am.
3. I like to know how to get from where I am to where I am going.

The third reason is of particular importance to those who are restless and want to change course. But to understand the significance of the third we need to appreciate the value of the first two.

1. Know where you are going

Navigation requires a bearing, a destination. Sometimes, the objective is clearly in view, while at other times it is obscured by bad weather or giant obstacles, yet still mysteriously lures us towards it.

To successfully change life's course, you must know where you want to go. Your goal should not be merely a greater level of income or a higher qualification. Dig deep and ask: how do you want to see yourself? A vision of the future, if it is to be a powerful force that pulls you further and higher than you have ever been before, has to be rooted in your desire to redefine yourself.

When I began my journey of personal transformation, I reached into my soul and my past, attempting to recapture the vision of myself I had had as a youngster. That image of an adventurer, an activist, or an advocate was far removed from the person I saw in the mirror. What I saw was someone overweight, sick, short of money, overworked and a slave to others. I was steadily resigning myself to be forever what I saw in the mirror, and that resignation led to a sadness of the soul. I wanted to regain personal liberty and dignity, and physical, spiritual and relational health.

How about you? What dreams have you relegated to the impossible, believing it is too late to realize them? Does that resignation make you sad? It is not too late to recover the vision of yourself that formed when you were young.

2. Know where you are

To know where you want to go is not enough to get you there.

I have met a lot of folks who are dreamers. They are always and predictably optimistic about their chances of succeeding, but they never advance. The reason for this is that they have not gone on to step two: honestly assessing where they are now.

Dreams are not reality. But to see our dreams become real, we need a map – not just to identify our destination, but to identify where we are starting from. My car's navigational system helps me in this regard. It is easy to get lost in the maze of Japanese streets. I can clearly see on my hard-copy map where I want to be, but my navigational system goes one step better: it actually pinpoints where I am. Often I am surprised when I find out how close I am to my destination. Other times, I should add, I am shocked by how far away I am. But even then, I am comforted by knowing the truth.

I have a problem with my weight and must be mindful of what and when I eat. Once or twice a month I weigh myself to see how close I am to my optimum weight. I've learned that I cannot trust what I see in the mirror or how I feel, for what I see, and what I feel, are often dictated by my mood. The digital scale provides me with an objective opinion.

One of the great quotes of Jesus Christ is: "You shall know the truth and the truth will set you free." Most sermons I have heard from this text have interpreted it as referring to Christian doctrine. In other words, "If you believe the right thing you will be set free." But in fact, all truth is liberating. If you want to see your dream come true, face the truth and be set free from a false sense of optimism. There is a more credible and durable optimism experienced by those who not only dream, but dare to face the truth of how distant those dreams are. It is when we have fixed these two points of reference – where we are and where we want to be – that we can begin to plot a course. This is when the fun starts.

3. Know how to get from where you are to where you are going

I am not sure who is more boring: optimists who never face the truth of how far they are from their goal, or pessimists who have given up because their dream seems too far from their present reality. I like to be with people who, when looking at their map, clearly know where they want to go, have honestly assessed where they are, and have plotted a course, or courses, to get from where they are to where they want to be.

Pragmatism and innovation are needed at this point, as there is more than one route available to us and sometimes what seems from our current vantage point to be the obvious way forward can turn out to be a cul-de-sac. In this case, we are required to retrace our steps ... but we are all the richer for the experience. So, while it is imperative to reconnoitre and plan, flexibility is needed in choosing the route. Sometimes, not only is the route redefined but so is the goal, for as we get closer to the horizon, we often discover that the horizon we have fixed is actually a step towards something greater and grander beyond.

The other day I was talking with a man who is a successful entrepreneur. He started his working life in a large corporation, but his dream was always to start his own company that targeted corporations as clients. He realized early on that he would not understand his customers unless he was one of them. After graduation from university he worked for five years within a corporation to learn how his "future customers" thought. He went on to start his own company, which he sold a handful of years later for $58 million. Today he is a venture capitalist, investing in start-ups. He does not do it for the money but because he gets a thrill out of using his money to empower others. At a recent breakfast meeting at the American Club in Tokyo, he told me that he is not impressed by people who have a great vision or unique idea.

"There is no shortage of good ideas," he stated. "But what impresses me is the person who knows how to turn those ideas into reality."

A management consultant in the UK told me: "The people who make successful entrepreneurs are not the visionaries but the individuals who get a buzz out of converting a good idea into an operational success."

But we are getting ahead of ourselves. Let's accept that you are about to begin your journey of personal transformation. Take time to discover your deepest, hidden dreams. You will not have to wonder about this too much; think back to when you were young, and write down how you viewed yourself as an adult. In other words, what dreams did you have then? What dreams do you have now? I have provided a dialogue box for you to write down the words that describe that youthful – or current – vision.

Next, write down the words that describe where you are now. How do the two images compare? Finally, take a few moments to write down the first steps you can take to move from where you are to where you have always wanted to be.

Executive summary

Maps are important in determining how to change and re-invent yourself.

1. Develop a vision of where you are going.
2. Assess where you currently are.
3. Examine all the possible routes to get from where you are to where you want to go.

All three steps are important. Dreams and reality checks are not enough. You must eventually use your map, stand up and start walking! Sometimes, we are not fully certain of the exact direction of our goal. Many a road is long and winding. Some routes will end up in failure – but this is part of the fun. Failure is not an obstacle; it is a necessary part of the journey.

Action plan

1. Have a retro-dreaming session. This is perhaps best done with the help of childhood friends and family, when you go back to the dreams of childhood and write down what you wanted to be when you grew up. Do not simply rehash what you used to tell adults when they asked you, but try to recover the images you had of yourself, when you imagined as a child what you would be when you were older. You will find the seed of the dreams of destiny.
2. List the dreams that you now have, and what in your heart of hearts you would like to achieve in the next ten years.
3. Assess your current position in life and try to determine the distance between your dreams and your current reality.
4. Brainstorm ideas and routes for what has to be done to achieve your goal. Do not let practical matters inhibit

you at this stage. Identify as many different options as possible.

Dialogue box

Key dreams:

1.

2.

3.

Current reality:

1.

2.

3.

Steps to be taken:

1.

2.

3.

Caution box

Don't over-plan. Drifting can add to the adventure. Leave space for the unexpected. Let your plans breathe.

Off to Africa

Jud lost all sense of time exploring the map room. Robert and Sarah had stayed with him for a couple of hours, wandering the halls of the famed institution, often silent as they examined the artefacts and photos of the explorations that had begun there. Then they had had to leave, but not before procuring a promise from Jud to keep them posted. About 30 minutes before closure, Jud sat down in the tea room and opened up the smaller envelope that had been inside Envelope 1.

Son,

I hope the maps in this grand place have given you a fresh sense of how large and diverse the world is: there is so much to discover.

Please be mindful of two things. First, travel at your own pace but remember you must rely on my money and not yours. This will force you to be resourceful and hopefully help you resist the temptation to escape from the adventure by going first class. Second, you need to be fit. I don't mean super-fit, but the level of fitness that comes from a lot of walking. Try to walk at least two hours a day, but some days walk eight or more. You will know why later. Your first destination is Kenya. Open Envelope 2 within an hour of landing at Nairobi Airport.

Enjoy the journey,
Dad

2. Love

"The great tragedy of life is not that men perish but that they cease to love."

Somerset Maugham, British playwright and novelist

"If I have a faith that can move mountains, but have not love, I am nothing."

St Paul in his letter to church members in Corinth

Numb in Kenya

The overnight flight from London to Nairobi had been uneventful. Jud had deliberately placed Envelope 2 deep in his carry-on bag, which he placed in the overhead compartment. He had never been to Africa before and as far as he knew neither had his dad. He was tempted more than once to get the envelope and read what it had to say. It seemed silly to wait for an hour before landing, but he decided to adhere to the instruction from his father.

Finally, the time came and Jud grabbed his bag from the overhead bin, and took out the envelope. He stared at it blankly for a moment and then opened it. Inside, there was a smaller sealed envelope with a message written on the outside:

> **Jud, when you arrive at Nairobi, take the next available flight to the north of Kenya, to a place called Lokichoggio. You will stay there only three to four hours and then return to Nairobi on the same plane. As soon as you arrive, open this envelope and I will tell you why you are there. Dad**

After clearing customs and immigration, Jud went to airport information and asked where he could book a flight to northern Kenya. He was told the only aircraft were small planes flown by aid agencies for the purpose of shuttling supplies, but they were willing to take paying passengers. He was directed to an office at the front of a small hangar. A woman ploughing through a tall pile of papers told Jud to talk to the pilot who was outside fuelling the plane.

"Yep, there's room, but it ain't cheap and we leave in about 45 minutes," the pilot said with a smile. "Go back to the office and tell Rhonda I said it was OK, and she'll relieve you of your money. Then come back and give me a hand loading the boxes."

Jud sensed the pilot was happy to have some company. He did as he was told, and was surprised by the cost – he hoped his dad had taken this extravagance into account.

Every item was weighed before being placed on board the small plane. Even Jud, the only passenger, had to step on the scales. "Yikes," he whispered. He was two pounds heavier than when he left the States just a few days before. "Must have been the London food," he said to himself.

A few moments later, they were in the aircraft, with engines revving. Jud, who had squeezed into the seat next to the pilot, watched with boyish fascination as the pilot methodically went through a checklist to ensure that all aspects of the plane were working properly. After a few minutes they were given the go-ahead from the control tower, and taxied out to the runway.

Despite being fully loaded, the plane made a speedy take-off and in just a handful of seconds was airborne. Jud felt his body compress into the seat with the sudden acceleration and lift-off. His eyes were wide open and his mouth drawn tight as the plane lurched into the hot, humid air coming off the African plain.

"It's the STOL kit," the pilot said unexpectedly.

"What?" Jud retorted, not knowing what on earth the pilot was talking about.

"Short Take-Off and Landing kit. We don't need it so much here in Nairobi, but for some of the strips we fly to, it's a necessity."

"I see," said Jud. His economy of words did not convey his excitement or his fear. It had been years since he had been in the cockpit of a small plane and he was aware of every jolt of the craft and action of the pilot. Jud's job required him to fly a lot but he never felt nervous on a commercial flight, which seemed to him like simply sitting in a large, cylinder-shaped waiting room, experiencing a moderate amount of ease, even boredom. But in a small aircraft Jud was excited by an odd mixture of a fear of heights and a love of flying.

The plane banked north and climbed to 10,000 feet. It wasn't long before Jud's head began to ache.

"This is the highest we can go without oxygen," the pilot explained.

The pilot seemed happy to talk most of the way and Jud was happy to listen, secretly hoping that he might be offered a few minutes at the controls. No such luck though, and Jud soon resigned himself to enjoying the changing scenery below. Soon the

*lush hills surrounding the Rift Valley gave way to the brown dust
of northern Kenya.*

*"We're entering Turkana territory," the pilot said. "The
Turkana are a nomadic tribe living at the cross-section of three
countries: the Sudan, Ethiopia and Kenya. War and famine have
wreaked havoc on their population, customs and dignity. They
and other tribes in the region have been the focus of aid agencies
for years."*

*After they landed, the pilot told Jud that it would take at
least three hours before the plane was ready to return to Nairobi.
Jud walked away from the plane in search of shade, which he
found by the back wall of a tin shelter made out of Coca-Cola
signs. He bought a bottle, sprang the cap off it and sat down,
leaning his back against the hut and taking several gulps of the
warm, wet drink. He took the small envelope from his shirt
pocket. Inside he found a note along with a photo of his dad
unloading aid from an aircraft. On the back of the old photo was
written one word: "WHY?"*

*A whirlwind spun past, giving momentary relief from the
flies that were fascinated by Jud's ears and eyes. The note flut-
tered in the wind. Jud grabbed it with both hands.*

>   **Dear son,**
>   *I visited this godforsaken place as a university student,
>   during the height of a famine. I took a semester off to help an
>   aid agency bring food to the Turkana people who were starv-
>   ing to death. I did it more out of a sense of adventure than
>   for any altruistic motive. But when I arrived, I was shocked
>   by what I saw. I witnessed not only death and starvation but
>   the undignified herding of thousands of people into a large
>   corral made out of a bush that looked like coiled barbwire.
>   Then, one by one, as if they were cattle, they were told to exit
>   through a narrow passage where they would be given their
>   ration of food. It seemed inhumane and very distant from
>   the comforts of your grandparents' home where I lived.*
>   *One day, a mother came to me and held her starving
>   child in one arm close to my camera. I didn't know what she
>   was doing at first. I wondered if she was asking me to take*

the child, which looked dead, but then I noticed a faint heaving of its chest. It took a moment before I realized what the mother was doing. She was offering me a chance to take a picture of her child in return for food. Just the day before, a television crew from an American church had arrived and while the cameras whirred, the crowd jostled to get in front of the lens. Food was handed out, but only to those on whom the cameras focused.

It was here that I had a crisis of faith that left me confused and puzzled. I tried to convince myself that the affairs of Africa were none of my business and beyond my control. It took a long time, but eventually I realized I was wrong. To be human is to care.

It seems unfair, but I want you to be as troubled as I was. Let this place break your heart. Human life and dignity are sacred gifts; this place reminds us of what we should not tolerate. It took me too long to concede that I had a responsibility. If I had only done so sooner, I might have redirected my life earlier than I did ...

Lovingly,
Your father

PS Do the flies still buzz around in gangs?

Tip 2: Locate love and you will find authenticity

The scene is a famous one. Scarlett O'Hara's neck stretches passionately upwards, her penetrating eyes pleading with the man who is both her saviour and her nemesis. The calm and handsome Rhett Butler, delighting in her vulnerability, looks down on her and utters the immortal words: "Frankly, my dear, I don't give a damn." His love of life, focus on self, and autonomy adds to his mystique and appeal. He is the rogue that moviegoers have admired for generations and some have sought to emulate. His declaration to Scarlett has become a dictum for many: If you want to get ahead, watch out for Number One and let no one get the emotional upper hand.

The term "principle of least interest" has been bandied about in academic circles for the past 75 years; it suggests that the person who has the least interest in a relationship has the most power. It makes sense. If a husband is hopelessly in love with his wife, but she is ambivalent, it is obvious who has the most power in the relationship. But this theory violates the basic premise of being human – we were born to care!

In the early 1990s, I travelled often in Bosnia-Herzegovina, attempting, along with others, to support children caught in the swirling chaos of social breakdown brought on by the war in the Balkans that violently tore neighbourhoods apart. I had lived in a war zone before, yet I was unprepared for the numbing darkness that had overcome the beautiful land of Bosnia-Herzegovina. One day, in search of advice, I asked one of the United Nations peacekeepers how they coped with the ethnic cleansing, mass rape and genocide that they had witnessed.

"You have to turn down your emotional volume. You cannot afford to care," he replied.

The principle of least interest seems sensible in conditions where one has to perform a professional duty, and when all around there is pain and suffering. But there is a problem: humans were designed to care. It is in our DNA. We need to care and history illustrates that the people we admire are those who paid a high price for caring: Martin Luther King, Nelson Mandela, Mother Teresa, Mahatma Gandhi, Jesus. We were created for love.

Stephen Covey, who wrote *The Seven Habits of Highly Effective People*, has since added "The Eighth Habit". Many people become effective but only a few attain true greatness, Covey maintains. His eighth habit is "Love: seeing and delighting in the potential of others".

My brother is a professional actor. Once, on the set of a TV series he was appearing in, he sought the advice of a famous actress of an older generation. The woman was the star of a hit comedy series. During a scene change, my brother summoned the courage to strike up a conversation. The actress's words and body language made him feel safe in her presence. She was not the prima donna he had expected. Towards the end of the conversation, he asked her for an acting tip. He has never forgotten what she said: "In every scene, every script, ask the question: "Where is the love?"

He did not understand the advice at first but as the years progressed it became the single most valuable acting tip he had heard. He has discovered that when you find the love, you find a source for your authenticity and authority as an actor.

It is an imperative: to embrace your future and realize your dreams, you must care. Is there a price to pay? Yes, of course, but love rejects the principle of least interest and in its place accepts vulnerability. There is risk, but the old adage, "Nothing ventured, nothing gained" is true. What blocks us from caring is the fear of being disappointed: of having our love rejected and refused.

John Lennon wrote, "All you need is love." It is a simple but profound truth. We need to take off the spectacles of power and instead look at the world around us through the lens of love. The 20/20 vision of love ensures a better perspective of ourselves, our families, our environments and our world. Love is more than a warm, fuzzy feeling resulting in an occasional glow. It affects our choices, and what we do with our time. There are four manifestations of love:

1. *Curiosity:* an irrepressible urge to discover things.
2. *Celebration:* despite the suffering around us, love compels us to find light in the darkness.
3. *Community:* love values connection. I like the quote of the Hopi Indians: "Joy is a raindrop landing in a river."
4. *Compassion:* love enables us to weep with those who weep, and laugh with those who have reason to laugh.

These four expressions of love make for a well-rounded, rewarding life.

Love is critical to all of life's decisions. It keeps us from being selfish while at the same time compelling us to love ourselves and our own life to the full. You can only live your life, no one else's. Therefore it is not a selfish thing to love your life. But as you develop passion for your own wholeness and well-being you will develop the same for others. It is imperative, therefore, that all of life's choices must be based on love.

My brother sought the advice of an actress. When I was 18, I summoned the courage to ask advice from Dr Bob Pierce, founder of World Vision, one of the world's largest development agencies. He said, "To be great, find out what is breaking the heart of God and pray that it breaks yours also."

I have not always followed it, but it is one of the best pieces of advice I have ever received. But love for others is only wholesome and healing if it stems from a legitimate love for yourself. Therefore the starting point for change, and personal re-invention, is the question: "Where is the love?" In other words, what are the things that I really care about in my life? What is it that I feel deeply for and have passion for? What is it that I really want to do? Once we have faced these questions honestly, then we must move on and ask, "How can I open myself up to others and care for them? How can I be faithful to myself while being faithful to the people around me?"

Viktor Frankl is an Auschwitz survivor who lost his wife in a Nazi death camp. As a doctor, his only way of escape from the surrounding terror was to care for his fellow inmates. In *Man's Search for Meaning* he wrote:

> Love is the highest goal to which humans can aspire, our salvation is through love. We all have choices in every situation. Even in terrible situations, we can preserve a vestige of spiritual freedom and independence of mind. Everything can be taken from a person but one thing: the last of human free-

doms – to choose one's own way. The essence of being human lies in searching for meaning and purpose. We can discover this through our actions and deeds, by experiencing a value and by suffering.

Executive summary

Love is the essential foundation from which to make all of life's decisions. To love is a matter of choice. Therefore everyone has the capacity to love.

1. Not to love is somehow subhuman. But to love is sometimes contrary to conventional wisdom.
2. To be great, one must love.
3. Love is divine. We all have it in us.

Action plan

1. Take a few moments and look at some of life's most difficult problems. Follow the advice of the experienced actress and ask the question: "Where is the love?"

2. Take each of the four manifestations of love mentioned in this chapter and do a self-assessment. On a scale of 1–10, with 1 being "not at all" and 10 being "very much so", ask yourself to what degree each of these attributes are expressed in your life:
    a. Curiosity: 1 2 3 4 5 6 7 8 9 10
    b. Celebration: 1 2 3 4 5 6 7 8 9 10
    c. Community: 1 2 3 4 5 6 7 8 9 10
    d. Compassion: 1 2 3 4 5 6 7 8 9 10

3. Finally, ask yourself the question: "How much do I love myself?" Enough to re-orient my life? This may seem selfish and egocentric but, unless we value ourselves, we cannot authentically value others.

Dialogue box

What do I have passion for?

1.

2.

3.

What impedes or numbs my love of self, family and the world?

1.

2.

3.

What could I do to foster a lifestyle of curiosity, celebration, community and compassion?

1.

2.

3.

Caution box

Loving others without first loving yourself can harm you and those near you. But authentic love stems from a belief in your own dignity and value which spills over to others.

Recovering in Nairobi

Jud felt guilty for being more interested in leaving Lokichoggio than in re-living his dad's experience. A waste of money, he thought. "All that expense in getting me to this godforsaken place, and I spend most of my time swatting flies."

He managed to talk with a few aid workers about the situation. While admiring their efforts, he became more depressed by their enterprise than encouraged by it. The fact that aid had become an industry since his father's summer there decades ago made Jud feel that the exercise of feeding starving people was futile.

The situation in Lokichoggio had improved since his dad's visit, but it was still a desolate place with no hope. Jud felt numb, tired, dirty and delighted when the pilot called him to board. The pilot was eager to take off quickly and sped to the midway point of the runway, where he turned the plane abruptly; in just a few seconds, the small craft was lurching upward into cooler air.

Jud slept or stared out the window for most of the return trip.

Back in Nairobi, he found a youth hostel, and after a cold shower in an outside cubicle, crawled into a vacant bed. He decided not to open the envelope marked 3 until the next morning. He was tired and wanted to sleep, but struggled to put the images of that day out of his mind.

3. Endurance

"Gambatte kudasai!"

Words of encouragement spoken by Japanese pilgrims
coming down Mt Fuji to those going up

Trekking in Tanzania

The sun rose in the eastern sky, bringing with it hot and heavy air. Jud slept soundly for six hours, before being awakened by a chorus of roosters. He was accustomed to a bit more luxury than the youth hostel offered, but there was a strange comfort to waking up in a room full of fellow travellers. Over breakfast he enjoyed listening to their tales and then, adhering to his father's instruction, set out for a two-hour walk. Jud knew that Nairobi was not the safest of places, yet the day was full of promise and he started his walkabout feeling only a trace of nervousness. Mid-morning, he sat down in the shade of a large, old tree, and opened Envelope 3.

>*Dear son,*
>
>*Your next stop is Tanzania, where you will do something I have always dreamed of: you will climb Mt Kilimanjaro. I advise you to book yourself on an expedition rather than make a solo attempt. There are lots of companies to choose from, all of whom will provide you with guides and the necessary equipment. Friends who have done it have recommended the Umbwe route, which takes about six days, including an overnight stay in the crater. Your biggest challenge may be the altitude: the summit is nearly 6,000 metres.*
>
>*I first heard of Kilimanjaro when I was a boy and I dreamed of climbing her ever since. Killy, as the mountain is affectionately known, is Africa's highest peak and the world's largest free-standing mountain. I hope to realize my dream vicariously through you. It will not be easy, but do your old man a favour: climb her for me.*
>
>*Love, Dad*

"Thanks, Dad ... thanks a lot." Jud was not impressed. He was never much of a climber and his dad knew it. They had climbed a couple of mountains together when he was a kid but Jud found the exercise tedious and exhausting. But since his dad was paying and it was part of his father's last will and testament he knew he had to do it. Back at the hostel, Jud found a leaflet offering various "Killy Packages", and within an hour all the arrangements were made. He had a week to enjoy Kenya before flying to Moshi, the nearest airport in Tanzania to Killy.

Over the next few days, Jud fitted in all he could. He visited the Rift Valley and marvelled at the vast flatness of the valley floor and the proud and colourful Masai people who inhabited it. He particularly enjoyed the wildlife of a game ranch he visited just outside Nairobi. He considered travelling to the beach resort of Mombasa for a couple of days, but decided against it. Going to the coast would not help prepare him for the high-altitude trek he was about to undertake. No matter what the day's itinerary was, Jud made sure he walked for two to four hours each day.

He found himself warming to the prospect of climbing Mt Kilimanjaro, a hope which was partly fuelled by conversations with people who had either climbed the famous mountain or decided against it.

"It's a hell of a high mountain," declared an Australian. "I did it in '95 ... was sick as a dog when I got to the top. Spent my 20 minutes there, vomited, held my aching head, which was banging like a drum, and then made a hasty descent back to where I could breathe."

"A climb that gets stuck in your memory, like a fly in porridge," said a woman from Kentucky. "Make sure, though, to go at your own pace. Don't let the tour operator push you too hard."

A tiny British woman from the Cotswolds, about 65 years old, said she had climbed it ten times. Her parents had lived in Tanzania for many years and Killy had always been part of her life. "When you get to the top, take a moment, and ponder your life," she advised. "There is a wonderful magic in reaching the top. The sight of the vast horizon through the clear, clean, rarified air opens you up to the world of possibilities. Life's everyday worries and pressures seem to slide into their rightful place. From the top of Killy, you can see the world and just maybe, if you're lucky, you will see your future."

When the time came to board the plane for Moshi, Jud's reluctant resignation had given way to excited anticipation.

Tip 3: There is power in perseverance

You're probably thinking, "I know perseverance is important, but I've heard all this."

But wait, if you skip this section you will miss an important insight that is fundamental to the whole book. So bear with me as I set the scene, before sharing with you a "not-so-secret" secret.

Half a century ago, so the story goes, on a stage in Oxford, a plump man with a liking for cigars shuffled up to the podium to make an address. His name was Winston Churchill and the assembled students and faculty were eager to hear what he would say in his commencement address. Winston Churchill had achieved a lot, but at a great cost. Whether trying to master English as a failing student, or standing fast during the Second World War, Churchill had demonstrated grit and determination. Students and faculty alike were in awe of him.

Churchill leaned his cane against the podium, placed his top hat on a small table, and took the cigar out of his mouth. Slowly he rose onto his toes and leaned forward. Looking around the great hall, he uttered three words three times, each time with a different emphasis.

"NEVER give up."

"Never give UP."

"NEVER GIVE UP."

His heels returned to the ground, he placed his cigar back in his mouth, picked up his top hat, and, with the aid of his cane, shuffled offstage. For a moment the audience was left in stunned silence, not only by the brevity of the speech, but by its profundity. As Churchill disappeared from view the auditorium burst into appreciative applause. He need not say any more – his life and achievements filled his words with authority.

No doubt the story has been embellished over the years but the fact that his speech has become legendary shows how much it stirs the soul.

When my sons turned ten, we climbed Mt Fuji, Japan's highest and holiest mountain. It is not a technical climb, but it is arduous. If you can imagine six hours on a step machine, while breathing in a room with a diminishing oxygen supply, you may get some sense of the tiring and tedious ascent. Yet tens of thousands climb it every year. On our way up, we met a never-ending stream of pilgrims coming down, and without exception, each one greeted us with the same words: "*Gambatte kudasai*", meaning "Stick at it" or "Keep going, please." In the group-oriented society of Japan, it is a greeting that is always given when meeting someone who is attempting a difficult endeavour. It is said with a tone suggesting: "For the sake of all of us, keep going." The words are spoken with a sense of appreciation and admiration, and in the belief that the goal is achievable.

Of course this is nothing new. We have been told all our lives that the tortoise won the race. It is the consistent, boring repetition of a task that achieves the desired goal. But the achievement of the goal is not the only reward that comes from persevering. Something more, something magical, something spiritual happens when we press on. An inner transformation takes place; we seem to enter a new dimension where fog gives way to clarity and we enter a state of heightened spirituality and awareness. It may only be subtle, but incrementally, each time you press on beyond what you believe to be a personal limitation, you are rewarded with bluer skies, greener grass and a clearer vision of what can be.

In Japanese, the word for "crisis" is comprised of two Japanese characters: one means "danger" while the meaning of the other is a blend of the English words "opportunity" and "promise". A feat of endurance, whether emotional, intellectual or physical, often involves a moment of crisis where you do not feel you can go on and your body says: "No more; that's enough." But often, the body is only responding to its known limits and past experience. This is where you have always stopped before and so the body naturally cries, "I haven't been beyond this point before. This is unknown; are you sure you want to go on?"

The cartoon character Homer Simpson has his own take on the concept and invented his own word to describe it: "crisi-tunity". Every crisis carries a challenging opportunity with it, and we can either quit or forge ahead. A new mindset must be created that maintains: "I will not give in to the pain." There is always the presence of danger when crisis and opportunity meet head on, but if you press past the pain, you are bound to experience that magical moment of something new. Like an eagle rising on a thermal, you discover a lift that raises you to a new perspective of yourself. But conversely, if a crisis is not created or forced, you will always tend to live within the assumed limits dictated by previous experience. Of course, sometimes pain comes from very real issues that are inflicted on us: a friend contracts cancer, a parent walks out on the family, or a child is killed in a car accident. These all cause pain, and it is important to feel the pain and experience it. But we will never move beyond the pain unless we make a decision to do so. It does come down to exactly that, to a choice: to move on, to survive, and to see a brighter day.

Many people assume that life can never change; they live within a prison of what has been. Dreams are suppressed and deemed unrealizable. But it is never too late to step out and embrace your future. It will take, however, discipline and stamina.

In the year 2000 I set out to ride my bike the length of Japan, intent on following the annual migration of the cherry blossoms. Cherry blossom season brings parties, lots of them, in the out-of-doors, where *sushi* is eaten and *sake* is drunk under the canopies of pink petals. I had a great time riding my bike 2,000 miles – the length of Japan – and enjoying the season's festivities. But it was not easy. More than I once I considered giving up. Homesickness, tendonitis, severe weather, news of family members involved in accidents ... these made the going tough at times. Once, I was arrested for inadvertently travelling where I should not have been. When I eventually arrived in Hokkaido I was elated and phoned my wife, leaving an exuberant message on the answering service. A week later, while cycling to the coast to catch a ferry and return to my home in Nagoya, I had an epiphany of sorts. I cycled down from the mountains on a quiet road through a still forest. The soft pounding of rain on my face as I descended stimulated the skin, and the knowledge that I had completed the journey I had set out to do caused my soul to glow. I felt at one with my bike and my surroundings. Here is how I describe the experience in my book, *Chasing the Cherry Blossom*:

> The forest was quiet around me, disturbed only by the swish of my wheels rolling over the moist surface and the soft crackle of rain hitting my rain gear. My spirit and mind became one and I wandered into my thoughts. It was the last day of travelling alone and I felt the inner glow of knowing I had achieved my goal. I had been enriched in so many ways but had the journey brought any insight into my mid-life status? Had I found any resolution to the questions about my life, past and future, that swam so often to the surface? Then it came, as clear as a whisper in a quiet room. It was a moment, spiritual in content and texture, but unaccompanied by strange or extraordinary signs. There was no booming voice from heaven and yet the words that came to my mind brought extraordinary clarity, unlocking and unleashing residual self-doubt. They came like a caboose at the end of a train of thought. As fleeting as the moment was, the words could not have come with such power and healing without the six weeks of pedalling that went before. In that moment, I saw clearly that the question haunting me was not as much a "Who am I?" as an "Is that it?" Are the major challenges of my life behind me? It was to this question, to this fear, that I felt the words that came to me were addressed.

> "Your challenges of the past will be eclipsed by greater challenges of the future. Your time is not over; it is yet to come. But you are in a special period, a period of privilege, where the challenge in your life is to love your wife, raise your boys and broaden yourself!"

I had cycled the length of Japan for these words.

One more thing about perseverance: it is a muscle that needs exercise to strengthen. My son and I learned an important lesson while mountain-biking a few years ago. We were on a double track in a forest near our home, cycling eight kilometres to the top. There were steep S-turns. Ryan was struggling, as a ten-year-old, and got off his bike at one point, wanting to give up. I felt bad for bringing him. A friend who was guiding us offered some advice.

"Ryan," my friend said, "there are three things you need to have to get to the top of this mountain. You have two of them already: a strong body and a good bike. But the mountain is conquered in the mind. You will go a long way in life if you learn to develop mental strength and stamina."

Ryan got back on his bike and rode to the top.

Recently, on my fiftieth birthday, my brother flew from Canada to join me on a celebratory 50-kilometre walk around Nagoya. He had done long-distance treks before, but never that distance. He was justifiably proud of himself when he finished in relatively good shape.

"Now that I know I can hack longer distances, I am going to increase the length of my cross-country treks," he declared proudly. It was not that he had become fitter physically, but he had become stronger mentally. It takes time, and like any strength training, we must go at it slowly and steadily, but our minds do get stronger with time and exercise.

Executive summary

The reward of perseverance or pressing on is not only in the satisfaction of achieving your goal, but also in the magic of a spiritual moment when we are lifted to a higher place: a place where clarity and creativity fuse and the soul is nourished.

1. Perseverance is essential to achieving any goal.
2. It often comes as a surprise but there comes a moment of "lift" when one presses on.
3. The muscle of perseverance has to be developed. It takes time to pass through all the incremental stages to reach your destination.

Action plan

1. Be inspired. Read a book about someone who accomplished a great thing. Pay attention to the moments where they chose to persevere in the face of difficult circumstances or opposition.
2. Reflect on your life and on any accomplishments that left you with an afterglow. What can you learn from them?
3. Set some very short-term goals that will stretch and exercise the mental muscle needed to persevere. Use those accomplishments to pursue longer-term goals.

Dialogue box

What motivates you?

1.

2.

3.

What causes you to give up on things?

1.

2.

3.

What steps can you take to strengthen the muscle of perseverance?

1.

2.

3.

Caution box

There are times when you must simply give in. The act of letting go of a dream, and of discontinuing the dogged pursuit of a goal, can liberate and renew you, and propel you in a new direction.

Exhilarated on Kilimanjaro

"YES!!!!" Jud screamed at the top. The climb up the mountain was sheer drudgery and at times excruciatingly painful. There had been more than one occasion when he wanted to give up. Had it not been for the cajoling and encouragement of others, he would have done so. His lungs craved oxygen, but the excitement of reaching the summit momentarily distracted him. The view was spectacular; the wide expanse of Africa was to be seen in every direction. Jud stood still and absorbed the moment, while slowly turning to take in the sight. The air was crisp and biting as it swirled around his face. The guide organized the obligatory photos and then told them it was time to descend into the crater, where they would set up camp and spend the night. It would take a few hours to get to the campsite.

Jud had naively thought that the downward journey would be a piece of cake. But he found it much harder than the ascent, particularly on his knees. He had foolishly opted for only one walking stick, and now he wished he had two. The climbers finally arrived at their destination, speedily set up camp in the mountain's core and ate supper, after which Jud retired to his tent. He fell asleep instantly. But sleep did not last long. He awoke three hours later with an overwhelming sadness that he did not understand at first. Was he just tired and hurting? As he became fully awake, he realized what it was: he was missing his dad.

"Damn you, Dad," he muttered. "Why are you doing this to me?"

He was missing Kathryn too. Even though he had kept in regular contact, sending email messages every time he could find a cyber café, Jud missed his wife. He could be at home in the comfort of his own bed, with Kathryn by his side and the dog on the floor. Instead, he felt overwhelmingly alone in his one-man tent, amidst a community of small tents at the bottom of the crater on Africa's tallest mountain.

"Damn you," he said again. Jud hated to cry, but the tears

were unstoppable. "Why did you have to die, Dad?" he whispered angrily so as not to disturb his fellow trekkers. "Why? Why? Why?"

The hot tears abated as the early morning grey that wrapped the sky like a dull, dirty blanket released shafts of early morning light onto the tent, brightening his small but private space. Feeling somewhat warmed by the early sun, Jud pulled out the envelope marked 4, and stared at it for over an hour. He was not sure he wanted to go on. What other cock-eyed scheme had his father dreamed up? His confusion as to whether or not to continue finally gave way to curiosity and he opened the envelope. Inside was a note along with two smaller sealed envelopes: one marked "Read in Dubai" and the other marked "Read in Singapore".

> *Dear son,*
>
> *Congratulations. I assume that you have completed the climb of Killy. If you didn't make it to the top, I admire you for trying. I wish I could be with you, son. To travel is to change. But change does not come without a cost. It can be difficult, yes, but it is also exhilarating.*
>
> *You are now going to a very different part of the world. There is something primeval about Africa, something basic and raw. It is a continent darkened by poverty. You are now going to Asia, where development has been excessive and riches are abundant. You have caught a glimpse of how large the world is from the top of Killy. You are on your way to another place to show how large and diverse the world is: Singapore. But I want you to route yourself through Dubai and ensure that you have at least three hours in the transit lounge there.*
>
> *I am proud of you.*
> *Dad*

4. *Geography*

**"I've always been inspired by the process
of travel: it opens your eyes to things that are
all around you at home but things that
you take for granted."**

Pico Iyer, a writer born in India, schooled in England,
raised in California and currently living in Japan

Flying to Singapore via Dubai

Jud was puzzled. But there was no good reason to discontinue following his father's plan now; he was in too deep. So, once back in Nairobi, he dutifully booked his flights to Singapore via Dubai.

The lavish transit lounge in Dubai amazed Jud; the restaurants and line-up of shops rivalled any shopping mall in the world, plus there was a hotel, a swimming pool and a fitness centre. Jud meandered around, at first dazzled by the array of things for sale, but becoming more interested in the sights and sounds of people on the move. Most travellers he would see only once; some he would see several times.

He considered paying $30 for access to the business lounge, but hesitated, as it might violate his father's instructions. The thought of sitting down in the quiet, luxurious lounge was luring and he reasoned within himself: "What difference would it make? After all, the whole airport is like a business lounge. We are all waiting, putting in time. The airport itself is not the final destination for any one of us; it is simply a transit area for people moving on."

Jud kept walking. He developed a fascination for passport control and the sight of people having their passports stamped and bags checked. Most travellers passed through speedily, while others received greater scrutiny. Some were led down mysterious corridors: it made Jud feel nervous and unsettled.

His flight was called and as he was settling into his seat he felt as if he had forgotten something. He rummaged through his pack and checked everything was in its place: ticket, passport, travellers' cheques, wallet, the remaining envelopes, etc. "That's it!" he said out loud. "The envelope I'm supposed to read in Dubai."

> **Dear son,**
>   **A transit lounge is a crossroads. It reminds us that the world is big and there are many directions you can travel.**
>   **For many years I kept going in the same direction. Somewhere along the way, I adopted the misguided notion that life is determined for you, and once you are on a path**

there is no stepping off. But when your mother died, my life was disturbed and I was forced to question where I was going. It was actually while sitting in an airport terminal staring at the departures board that I realized the future was in my hands. I was scared and optimistic at the same time. I knew I had the power to choose where I wanted to go.

I deeply regret that your mother is no longer with me, but I am grateful that her last gift to me was an awakening: she let me see that life had much to offer me and I had much to offer the world.

I have gone on too much, please forgive me. But I hope you are experiencing what I am trying to say. Jud, you have the power to choose your life's course. Don't settle for drift; reach for your dreams.

Have a good flight.

Dad

PS When you arrive in Singapore, keep walking with your eyes wide open to the world around you.

Jud landed at Changi Airport in Singapore and made his way through passport control. As he walked through the terminal he noted that while the design and layout were different, there were subtle similarities between Changi and Dubai. He even recognized a few familiar faces.

Once through immigration he took a taxi downtown. The subway was cheaper, but he wanted social contact, someone to talk with. Besides, taxis, he discovered, were cheap here compared to places like New York and London. The instructions were clear: "Go downtown and walk and observe." The plan was to spend at least two nights in this remarkable city, and as luck would have it, Jud arrived as the Chinese New Year was in full swing. Rather than check into a hotel, Jud asked the taxi driver where the best place to experience the New Year celebrations was.

"Chinatown, of course!" declared the taxi driver.

Jud felt foolish. "Of course," he replied. "Take me there."

"OK!" said the driver. "You lucky."

"Lucky? Why?"

"This is best night of the New Year."

"Oh ... why?"

"Everyone is having reunion dinners," explained the taxi driver. "Reunion dinner is when whole family gets together for tradition meal before going to parties on the streets."

"Are you going to a reunion dinner?" Jud asked.

"Of course, but first I make money."

"What time will you eat?"

"About eight o'clock!"

The taxi driver dropped Jud off at the edge of Chinatown and he walked through the narrow streets. He enjoyed the cacophony of tropical sights, sounds and smells; the aroma of fruit and spice fused together, lingering pleasantly in the hot, moist air. Everywhere, people were drinking tiger beer and eating New Year cookies, and tailors were selling suits.

Jud kept walking, out of Chinatown towards the quay. Here he passed waterfront pubs where crowds of white faces and white shirts gathered at the end of the trading day. "If it wasn't for the heat and the smells, I'd swear I was in London or New York," he thought.

He strolled by statues of Europeans who had shaped Singapore, men like Joseph Conrad and Alexander Laurie Johnston, the first chairman of the Chamber of Commerce. Jud stopped for a few moments in the shade of an underpass where a group of dancers were rehearsing. Finally, after several hours, and feeling hungry, he sat down at a Thai restaurant by the Esplanade and ordered dishes he had never heard of before but which caught his fancy. He feasted on tom tu talay, seafood soup, and barbecued chicken with Thai plum sauce.

Tip 4: Changing places can be the catalyst for personal transformation

Not too long after I turned 40, I made one of the singularly most significant decisions of my life: to follow my wife and relocate my family to the other side of the world. My life in the UK was full, but full of the same stuff: meeting after meeting after meeting, often with 100 motorway miles between them. Most days I left home before my family woke and returned long after the family had fallen asleep. My health was unsteady and my marriage was stale. I was growing numb. Passion was waning and I often woke feeling depressed and disappointed.

Then an opportunity came to move to Japan. The Japan option did not come out of the blue. My wife, Kande, was born and raised in Japan. The daughter of Canadian missionaries, Kande left Japan when she was 17 but always dreamed of returning. During our courtship, we agreed that once we were married she would follow me from Canada to the UK, putting my interests first, but some day I would follow her to Japan and put hers first. I felt good about the agreement, as a 1980s male, but, to be frank, I never thought it would happen. Japan was too far, too strange and too expensive to be a viable option. But in 1995, we took that option, and my life has never been the same. Not only did my lifestyle change, but I changed. I woke up.

You see, an extraordinary thing happens when you move into a new land, a new culture and a new life: your senses come alive. For me, they went into overdrive.

I had grown numb to the world around me. The familiar had become invisible. But the strangeness of a new land excited and aroused me, and I found myself getting up early to explore. My first adventure was to walk to the top of the hill behind our new home. Once at the crest, I scoped the city, examining its topography and key landmarks. I looked in the other direction towards the mountains and enjoyed the view of the Japanese Alps sparkling with fresh snow. I was like a boy in a candy store. Everything looked so different, and I swore that I would explore this new land, intellectually, spiritually, socially and physically. I made two commitments to myself:

1. Become less dependent on a car, and more dependent on self-propelled transportation.
2. Throw away my diary. Rather than carve up my week into fifteen-minute segments, I would only take on as many commitments as I could actually remember without writing them down.

Within six weeks I had a bicycle on which I explored the city and the countryside, and commuted to the language school in which I had enrolled. Within months, I set my sights on cycling the length of Japan. And for the most part I was surviving without my diary! Changing places seemed to rewire me. I found a new rhythm.

I know what you may be thinking: "I see your point, but changing places does not change who you are."

You are right. The old saying is true: no matter where you go, there you are. Long after the wonder of a new place wears off, you are still stuck with you. Old issues and characteristics will resurface. But my point is that a move, new stimuli, new sensory experiences, do not so much change you, as ignite parts of you that had gone cold or dormant. Yes, the answer is within yourself, not in your environment, but a change of places awakens the deep inner self, as it confronts and enjoys new sensory stimulation.

Frances Mayes, the writer of *Under the Tuscan Sun*, said a similar thing of her move to Italy from California. She found her writing was not so much renewed as it was reformed: "... the place changed the rhythm in my brain and I could no longer write in lines. I was writing in sentences. That was a very big difference to me. So when I changed my life, I changed my form." I am an advocate of changing places: not only because it stimulates our senses, but because it broadens the horizon of our lives.

Pico Iyer, staff writer for TIME magazine and acclaimed author, speaks of a new breed of human being: a "global soul". People with a global soul are comfortable anywhere in the world. They are restless – and are enlivened by new experiences and places. The sense of newness can last for years, even decades, because curiosity and a sense of adventure is a state of mind. Some would say that global souls get bored too easily, but quite the opposite is true. They establish roots wherever they are and remain rooted even if they move on. They are motivated by a love of life and sense of adventure in discovering all that the world has to offer.

Both my sons have become global souls. Educators call them "third-culture kids". This designation has sometimes been used to describe the children of missionaries and expatriate workers, who experience particular problems: they are not part of their home culture nor are they part of their host culture; they, in fact, form a third culture. Maybe in the past this was a problem for kids, but today the third-culture kids are to be admired: they move easily through airports, cultures and languages. My older son's bedroom window faces the airport in Nagoya – the old airport, that is. A new one was recently built on a man-made island about 60 kilometres south of our home. At dinner, a few days after the new airport opened, my son commented that he missed watching the planes land and take off. He told us that often, against the backdrop of the setting sun, he would gaze at the planes coming and going, a reminder that anywhere in the world was only a few hours away.

Moving places is a great antidote to midlife drift. To those who feel that travel is a form of escape and a running away from real life, I have one thing to say to you: "Of course it is!" But what is wrong with that? Escape can be a good thing. If your life were in some sort of danger would you not try to escape? Wouldn't you take your family with you? To escape danger is sensible and good. On that premise, if your life is in danger of becoming monochrome, then why not move? Of course, wise planning is a must, as is due attention to your responsibilities towards those who love you and those to whom you have obligations, namely your employer and the tax man. Existing responsibilities must be taken seriously, but I contend that for many people, the only way to awaken dormant dreams is to change places.

Executive summary

Changing places is good for the soul. It forces your senses into optimum performance, and every little discovery, no matter how mundane, nourishes your excitement of life.

1. Spending time in an airport reminds us how big and full of opportunities the world is.
2. The nervousness that is felt travelling and moving across borders should not be seen as a warning of danger, but as a signal that a great adventure is about to be embarked upon.

Action plan

1. Make a list of the places you have always dreamed of visiting, but do not include the idyllic beach holiday. People who dream of beach holidays are usually dreaming of "rest". Quite simply, they are exhausted. Try to imagine places and experiences that will awaken you, not simply give you a rest.
2. Now ask yourself the question: What is stopping me from going there? Is it money? Is it obligations? Is it time?
3. You do not have to go far. As an experiment, walk through a neighbourhood that you usually only drive through. Take note of all that you see, hear and smell that you have never experienced before. Write down what you observed or sensed about the neighbourhood that you hadn't before.

4. Finally, ask yourself, "When was the last time I felt fully alive? When I was full of curiosity and celebration, feeling that I was part of something larger than myself?" Make notes of that experience and learn what you can from it.

Dialogue box

Places I like to visit:

1.

2.

3.

What is stopping me?

1.

2.

3.

What steps do I need to take, to reacquaint myself with the world around me?

1.

2.

3.

Alive at the Esplanade

Although physically tired, Jud was alert to the sights, sounds and smells that swirled around him. He missed Kathryn but was glad that he was where he was. Feeling content and restless all in the same moment, Jud decided that it was a good time to read the next message. He took another swig of his tiger beer and opened the envelope marked: "Read in Singapore".

> *Jud, welcome to Singapore!*
> *The first time I came here, I was wide-eyed and struck by the energy and diversity of this crossroads community. Singapore is a city of wonder, not only a natural wonder – its location near the equator is both strategic and spectacular – but also a cultural and historical marvel. Singapore is everywhere and nowhere. It is a microcosm not only of Asia, but of the world. This city was built on trade and has become a global marketplace. From Singapore you can see the world. Take a good look!*
> *Love, Dad*
>
> *PS Easy on the Singapore Slings.*

The sun was setting, casting a pinkish orange glow on the oddly shaped Esplanade building behind Jud. It was as if someone was manipulating dimmer switches. As the light of the sun slowly diminished as it sank below the horizon, the lights of the city began to twinkle in the encroaching darkness. A large freighter ploughed through the harbour in the twilight, causing barely a ripple in the calm waters. Jud closed his eyes and a gentle progression of images slid past his vision at about the same speed as the freighter: the pub in London, the map room of the Royal Geographical Society, the desolation of northern Kenya, the penetrating cold at the summit of Kilimanjaro, and now the colour and excitement of Singapore.

5. Money

"I will go to my grave claiming that the less you spend the more you enjoy, the more authentic the experience, the more profound, the more exciting, the more unexpected it is."

Arthur Frommer, publisher and travel writer

"You open yourself up to a country or to a person and you find in the opening more riches than you ever imagined."

Pico Iyer

Mindanao madness

It was Jud's first visit to Asia and he found the tastes, sights and sounds of Singapore breathtaking. The diversity of its people, the richness of its history, and the dynamics of its culture impacted him in a way that surprised him. He could not get enough.

On the third day, Jud rose early and walked to Orchard Road and beyond. He eventually found himself near the Raffles Hotel in the late afternoon and decided to treat himself to a Singapore Sling in the bar. He settled into a large rattan chair, with the cool, colourful drink in one hand, and the contents of Envelope 5 in the other.

Dear son,

The next phase of your journey will take you from Singapore, where wealth and prosperity is visible all around you, to a very different place where people live with much less: the southern Philippine island of Mindanao. I have a friend, a very good friend, who was a porter in the hospital where your mother was treated for cancer: his name is Roberto. He has returned to his home island to help his ageing mother and manage the family store and small travel company he started, called Davao Walking Tours. After your mother died, he invited me to join him on a one-week walking tour of Mindanao. The time I spent with him in the hills of Mindanao was a turning point. I returned home determined to lead a healthy and balanced life, chasing the dollar less, and reaching for life more. I gained a better perspective of myself and how the other half, or should I say, 90 percent of the world, live.

Just one thing, though. When you walk with him you are to take nothing with you, only a notebook and your malaria tablets. Roberto will supply everything else, although there will not be much else that you require. I mentioned to him that one day you might show up, so hopefully he will not be too surprised. I wrote his number on the back of this note.

Love, Dad

In the evening, Jud called Roberto. Roberto had heard of the death of his father through friends in the hospital, and expressed his sadness to Jud.

"I received a letter from your dad a few weeks ago," he said. "He told me of his plan to send you on a world adventure and asked if it was alright for you to visit me."

Jud sensed that Roberto was a compassionate man.

"You will need to spend one night in Manila," Roberto advised him, "but catch the first flight to Davao the next day. We will be in the hills for about a week but your journey will end on a beach."

"Sounds great," responded Jud. "See you in a couple of days!"

Tip 5: Money matters ... but not as much as you think

The correlation between the amount of money to spend and the intensity of the adventure is not as great as people think. Two travel writers from the 18th century, Alexander von Humboldt and Xavier de Maistre, illustrate for me the different approaches to travel and exploration.

Alexander von Humboldt wrote a book called *Journey to the Equinoctial Regions of the New Continent*, which chronicles his journey through South America. He spared no expense to make his trip. His entourage and equipment included:

- ten mules
- 30 pieces of luggage
- four interpreters
- a chronometer
- a sextant
- two telescopes
- a Borda theodolite (an instrument used to measure distances)
- a barometer
- a compass

- a hygrometer (an instrument for measuring humidity)
- letters of introduction from the king of Spain
- a gun

Another writer of the same period, Xavier de Maistre, born in the French Alps, did not believe that one had to travel far or on a big budget to be an explorer. His destination was his own room! The subsequent tome that he wrote was published under the title *Journey Around My Bedroom*. It was such a success that he wrote a sequel called *Nocturnal Expedition Around My Bedroom*. For the second expedition he went a tad further, concluding his journey on the window ledge. Unlike Humboldt's elaborate list of resources, Maistre required only a comfortable pair of pyjamas for his journey. Maistre recommended room travel to "the poor, and those afraid of storms, robberies, and high cliffs". He wanted to illustrate that a lack of wealth is no excuse if a person wants to be an adventurer and explorer.

I wrote a book some years back called *Boys Becoming Men*, in which I advocated the organization of adventures that would serve as a puberty rite of passage. After its release, several men wrote to me saying, "It's alright for you – you can afford it!" I was dismayed by their response for two reasons. First of all, our children are worth investing in. Second, it is a false assumption that adventures are expensive.

Money is important ... it makes the world go round: but it does not matter as much as some think. Here are two reasons why.

1. The power of the will
No, I am not talking about the preparation of a legal document (although every responsible adult should have one). I am referring to the amazing, even mysterious way in which humans can, by the power of choice, "will" something to be.

I was born into a travelling family. My father had an

inclination to announce, a year in advance, that the following year we would be in such and such a place, usually on the other side of the world. It always came to pass, even though at the time of the pronouncement no plans had been made or money saved. We children thought he was crackers when he made his declarations. But, lo and behold, we were in that country, enjoying that event a year later, just as he said we would. His philosophy was always: "What you say is what you get." And now, I am finding that Dad was not far off. I have those things happen too. I think about something challenging, and then I say: "I'm going to do that." As soon as I decide, things begin to fall into place and I am able to do it. That is probably the secret to accomplishing those things thought impossible: be decisive, exert your will, and go for it.

"I'm a big believer in will and its power," said Frances Mayes, who saw her dream of owning a home in Tuscany become a reality. "You have to trust your will. I believe in wrenching what you want out of whatever circumstance there is in front of you."

I have met folks time and time again who have done just that: they make a decision and then mysteriously an opportunity presents itself. The emotional timing was right, and so the plunge was taken.

2. Going first class is second rate
I have learned a lot of lessons from travelling. One of them is that the best trips are those where you stay clear of international resorts and those who stay in them. These places are often populated by tourists not really interested in exploration but opting for the security of familiar surroundings.

Five years ago, I realized a dream: I cycled the length of Japan. It took six weeks. I anticipated the joy of discovering Japan, but was surprised by the pleasure that I derived from living simply and cheaply for a month and a half. My entire belongings fitted into two small panniers (saddle bags). There is nothing like having to feel the weight of your belongings on a bicycle to help you reduce your luggage to the absolute essentials. I started out on the journey with three bags, but at the end of the first gruelling day of riding over 100 kilometres on a loaded bike, I reduced my needs even further, sending one of the bags home. And you know, it is the simple, unencumbered life that is the reality of most of the world's population, a point not lost on the great travel writer Arthur Frommer: "When you live lavishly you're really living a kind of life which only a small fraction of the world enjoys, and which is enjoyed primarily for reasons of social emulation. It took me a long time to realize that the rich folks in first class were not nearly as interesting to talk with as the people you ordinarily meet in tourist class or the breakfast room of a pension."

One of the great opportunities presented by making a move is the chance to clean out your garage, your wardrobe, your list of assets ... and to start over. It is liberating. When Kande and I first started talking of our move, we assumed that we would ship everything to Japan. But as the time got closer, we challenged every item we owned, asking whether it was essential to our lives in Japan. We ended up selling or giving away 95 percent of our belongings (including my library). The decision to liquidate our assets not only increased our cash supply (money is much easier to ship than a sofa) but also enhanced the sense that we were starting afresh: a cleansing of sorts.

Don't be greedy
My friend, James, told me a great a story that he heard from his father when he was a child. James has sought to apply the lesson of the story to his own life and business. Recently, he helped sell the business of which he is president for $25 million.

The story is about a young boy who everyone thought

was stupid. One day, during recess, a group of the lads decided to test his stupidity. They held out a 25-cent piece and a ten-cent piece and told him he could choose one and keep it. The boy chose the ten cents. The boys guffawed and called some other children over and repeated the exercise; again the boy chose the dime. At every recess for several months the same exercise was repeated and the boy became the subject of ridicule in the school. Eventually, the headmaster learned of the daily scorning and asked the boy why he allowed the kids to make fun of him; did he not know that a quarter was worth more than a dime? "Yes, I do," the boy said, "but if I took the quarter the first time, they would never have offered me money again."

James told me the lesson he learned from this story is not to be greedy. But there is another lesson too: When everyone else thinks you are an idiot for making the choices you do, your day of vindication will come.

I leave you with four principles for effective financial planning. These are not original, and if you want to explore them further, I recommend that you purchase a great book by Richard Foster called *Money, Sex and Power*. In the section on money, Foster offers great advice on how to manage money. You may be surprised that his source is the Bible. It has been years since I read his book, but I have developed these four principles from his writings:

Principle 1
Remind yourself that what you own is not really yours. You are only a temporary steward. One day you will die and your wealth will be left behind.

Principle 2
Fulfil your obligations to your country, your community and your family. In other words, pay your taxes and invest in your family.

Principle 3

Grow your money. Do not hoard and hide it, but invest it. Seek a return on your money. Some may be surprised that this principle is in the Bible. Jesus told a story about a master who gave his employees some capital to invest. He was dismayed by one of his men, who decided to protect the money and simply buried it until his master asked for it back. But another employee, who invested and grew the capital, was applauded.

Principle 4

Be generous ... give your money away. We must fulfil our obligations (Principle 2) and it is proper to see our money grow (Principle 3) but when we are generous with our money we are asserting that it does not belong to us in the first place, that we are only stewards. To give money away is to be liberated from its power.

Remember, you are not a slave to money: money should serve you. Discover the secrets of applying its energy.

Executive summary

There is simply no excuse for letting money or the lack thereof hold you back from redirecting all or part of your life. Wealth is relative. There will always be someone with more, and always many with less than you have. Be grateful for what you do have; use your resources wisely and you may find that you will spend less than you think.

Good and responsible planning is required to make a life change. And while money certainly helps, money is not, and must not be, the determining factor in our decisions.

1. Money is not the main reason why people hesitate to reach for their dreams. Rather, it's the lack of will.
2. Going first class is second rate.

3. Do not be greedy.
4. Abide by the four timeless principles of financial planning.

Action plan

1. Develop a balanced view of money. Do not let its power intimidate you. Read Richard Foster's *Money, Sex and Power*. Writing from a biblical perspective, Foster offers sound and ancient advice on financial management. For many years I lived in fear of money, but once I discovered it was a power to be subjugated, I learned to control it rather than let it control me.
2. Prepare a budget. Be brutal: ask if each item/expenditure is absolutely necessary to your objective. Also keep in mind that having a budget is not enough to have sound finances. Learn to understand the importance of cash flows, budgets and balance sheets.
3. Brainstorm what possible revenue streams you could maintain and what new revenue streams could be created.
4. Seek professional financial advice.
5. Have a garage sale and sell out. I have not met a family yet who, having brought everything with them to Japan, was glad they did. Most regretted not selling more of their belongings. Give your most treasured items as a long-term loan to close friends and family.

Dialogue box

What principles guide my financial management?

1.

2.

3.

How much would it cost to realize one or two of my dreams?

1.

2.

3.

Ideas I have to grow my money and/or create new revenue streams:

1.

2.

3.

Caution box

It is an old adage, perhaps so familiar that it has lost its edge, but it is true – "Money can't buy me love."

Mindanao

It was a remarkable week. Jud and Roberto trudged through the hills of Mindanao with only the clothes on their backs and a small rucksack each. They stayed most nights with the Lumad, the tribal people of Mindanao, who inhabit the picturesque countryside of hills, mountains and forests. The Lumad, Jud discovered, were experiencing change because of war, deforestation and the use of chemical fertilizers. Though he felt sad for them, he was struck by their contentment. To Jud they appeared poor, but he sensed that when they looked at him, they did not see Jud as someone wealthier than themselves, but simply as someone from a different place. Roberto too seemed a man who was content. Although he knew what America was like, and how much money could be made there, he was happy to be walking through the hills of his island home.

"I'm glad I went to America," said Roberto, "not because I was able to make more money, but the change helped me establish what was really important to me. What I missed most was my home, this island, with its natural surroundings. That's why, when I returned, I set up Davao Walking Tours to attract tourists. I want to do my little bit to help bring peace and prosperity to this wonderful place."

Jud discovered that Roberto was a keen environmentalist who was grieved by the years of conflict that had made many of the hills inaccessible. Even now, he had to be mindful of potential tensions and sometimes had to cancel a walk and return the money to his clients when security risks were too great. Roberto was also involved in a number of NGOs promoting sustainable agriculture and conflict resolution.

"Tomorrow is our last day, Jud," said Roberto, "and we're going to spend it in a village that has been working with an NGO for several weeks, capping a spring and laying three kilometres of pipe to bring clean, potable water into the village."

"Sounds interesting," Jud said.

"Tomorrow is the ceremonial turning on of the tap. Would you like to witness it?"

"Sure would," replied Jud.

The two men got up early the next morning and walked fifteen kilometres, arriving just before the water ceremony started. Roberto introduced Jud to the engineer who worked with a Manila-based organization assisting villages that needed accessibility to clean water. After greeting the village leaders, they retreated a discreet distance to observe the ceremony. There was dancing, offering of prayers, and then the climactic moment when the tap was finally turned on by an older woman of the village, selected for the honour. The villagers fell silent. All eyes were on the tap and the clean, sparkling torrent that gushed forth. The awed silence was broken by an unexpected shriek from the old woman whose hands were still on the tap. She suddenly lunged at the unsuspecting engineer and threw her arms around him, violating a tribal taboo that prohibited a woman from touching any man other than her husband. After a few moments she released her embrace and began to dance. Her demonstrative appreciation triggered an outpouring of thanks from the villagers who, one by one, passed their hands and sometimes their faces under the precious liquid that was still pouring from the tap.

Roberto leaned over and whispered to Jud that the women were shouting, "Once we were cursed, but now we are blessed." He explained that two weeks before, an elderly woman had died of suffocation while bearing a basket of water on her back from the water source, five kilometres away, that the village relied on. The strap over her forehead had slipped, instantly breaking her windpipe. Her death was a strange one, but was by no means the only water-related death in the valley. Ironically, the valley was called Pigbalowan, meaning "Word of God descended from Heaven".

"The spiritually inclined community should have felt blessed with such a name," explained Roberto, "but instead they felt cursed. Life was miserable. But now, with pure water readily available, the community's quality of life will be remarkably enhanced."

Later that night Jud lay on the wooden planks in a hut, with

Roberto snoring beside him. But he could not sleep. The sight of the celebration of the arrival of water, and the story of the old woman who had died just two weeks ago, stuck with him. It caused him to reflect on his own life, his job and his values. He was blessed indeed, but it was slowly dawning on Jud that any desired ascent up the corporate ladder, in pursuit of greater power and greater money, was misguided. "Sure," he thought to himself, "managers, leaders and CEOs are needed in the modern world, but to pursue these things, believing that they can somehow make life better, is perhaps a false assumption." What he had seen today illustrated that what matters most of all is life and dignity.

6. *Fitness*

"Health and cheerfulness mutually beget each other."

Joseph Addison, English essayist, poet and statesman
(1672–1719)

"Getting fit is a political act – you are taking charge of yourself."

Jane Fonda, movie star, political activist and fitness guru

Good times on the beach

Roberto and Jud returned to Davao by bus. About three kilometres from the city centre, Roberto announced, "This is where I get off."

"Huh?" Jud was surprised and a little concerned. "Just like that? You said we were going to a beach. Not that the beach is important, but this is rather abrupt, isn't it? Is something wrong? Have I done something to offend you?"

"None of the above," said Roberto. "You are going to the beach, but not with me. In the letter that your father sent me, saying that you might show up for a walking holiday, he gave me very clear instructions ... you are to go the beach on your own. You will spend two nights there. It's quite inexpensive. Once the bus gets to the city centre bus station, catch a taxi to the port. From there you will catch a water taxi to your hut where I have arranged for you to stay. You can swim, snorkel, even learn to scuba dive, but the beach and the water is not the place your father wants you to see."

Roberto's eyes twinkled with a mischievous sparkle, the corner of his mouth turning up in a wry smile. Sensing Jud's curiosity, Roberto added: "All will be revealed in the next envelope."

At that, the bus ground to a halt as though the bus driver knew that if Roberto said anything more, the surprise would be given away. From the front of the bus, Roberto shouted, "I'll pick you up in the port when you come back. Give me a couple of hours' notice though. Have fun!"

"Well, Dad, you certainly planned this out well," Jud muttered. "It's hard to believe that you were sick at all, having put this amount of thought into the trip."

A couple of hours later, Jud arrived at the beach hut. Considering the price, it was pleasant: spacious, aesthetically pleasing and only 100 metres from the beach. His was one of a dozen small cottages strewn through a grove of palm trees.

In his room Jud opened Envelope 6 and found two items: a short note, and a photo of his dad and himself taken a year before. The sight of his dad looking fit was a sad reminder that he was gone. "If only we had known that cancer would take him so quickly," Jud thought to himself. In contrast to his dad, Jud's image was not so complimentary. Sure, you could tell they were father and son; but in comparison to the older man, Jud was overweight and colourless, with stress lines accenting his forehead. His dad had a huge grin and rosy cheeks, and his eyes exuded a warm energy. Jud, on the other hand, looked weary, worried and worn. Jud tucked the photo into the top right corner of the mirror frame and unfolded his father's letter:

> **Dear son,**
>
> **You are probably curious why I brought you here. You are about to find out, but first I need you to get into your bathing suit ...**

"What in the world?" Jud asked himself. He was tempted to ignore the instruction and keep reading, but then felt that his dad was watching somehow, so he ripped open his rucksack and quickly changed into his bathing suit.

> **Son, have you done it? No cheating now! OK. I have a surprise for you. You will discover what it is when you look in the mirror.**
>
> **More later,**
> **Love, Dad**

Jud dropped the letter and faced the full-length mirror. It took a moment for him to figure out what his dad wanted him to see, but when he did, Jud smiled. Having just seen himself in the photo a few moments ago, Jud was expecting a near-naked version of the same slightly podgy body. But to the contrary, he saw a thinner, fitter, tanned version of himself.

"Wow," Jud said aloud. "I've lost weight and toned up without realizing it!" He looked healthier and leaner, and even stood straighter. A week of walking and eating healthy, organically-grown food had paid off.

But as Jud thought about it, he realized that his lifestyle had changed ever since he had started this harebrained adventure. He was walking long distances every day and eating fresh produce whenever possible. He had often complained to his dad that he did not have time to maintain a daily physical fitness regime. His dad never commented, but now posthumously, he had put his son on the road to fitness without the son realizing it. Jud smiled, grabbed a towel and headed to the beach.

Tip 6: Super-size your life, not your body

It is said that the fattest people on earth live in the UK and North America. A few years ago, it would have been politically incorrect to point this out, but the alarm has been raised and educators, parents, scientists and politicians are debating what can be done to curb the trend towards obesity. The rise of heart disease, diabetes and other fitness-related illnesses is rightly causing concern. I am neither a fitness expert nor a diet specialist. However, I believe that our level of fitness is a direct result of the choices we make. By making lifestyle choices and choosing to eat better and exercise more we will not only enhance the quality of our lives but extend them too.

Ten years ago, I was overweight and either sick or about to be sick. In my twenties, I ignored concerns about my health. I ate what I wanted, when I wanted, and exercise was sporadic at best. I regret that I did not get to know my body better and take my long-term health seriously, despite warnings which included contracting hepatitis from eating poorly, and the news that my father had been diagnosed with diabetes. It wasn't until my forties that I promised my wife that I would eat better and exercise more. I have learned a lot in the last ten years, but three discoveries have been particularly helpful. I wish I had made them sooner, much sooner.

Discovery 1. Adrenalin is great; endorphins are better
A few years ago I decided to use a bicycle more and a car less, at least for local transportation. I still recall the glow of my first three-mile ride. My bottom was sore, my back ached, but my mood had changed for the better. The next day, the three miles were extended to five, and then eight, and soon I was riding 20 to 30 miles a day just getting around and doing business. The bike soon became a companion and my preferred mode of transport. In the past ten years, I have ridden about 25,000 miles by bicycle. I am 25 pounds lighter, and whenever I feel stressed I hop on the bike and go for a ride.

My brother's doctor once told him, "If you are sweating, you are winning." The great thing is that you do not have to sweat to such a degree that it becomes uncomfortable: simply raise your heartrate to about 65% of its maximum and you can go for hours. I found that not only does a cardio workout help keep the weight down and the heart in good condition (if you exercise wisely) but it also results in mental benefits. John F Kennedy was right when he said that "Physical fitness is not only one of the most important keys to a healthy body; it is the basis of dynamic and creative intellectual activity". The reason for this is the release of tiny molecules called endorphins. Whereas adrenalin brings a tingle (and sometimes a hangover of sorts), endorphins bring a glow that creates a sensation of well-being. The amazing thing is that the more the receptors are stimulated by endorphins, the more sensitive they become and the easier it is for endorphins to stimulate them.

How are endorphins released into our system? Through exercise! When I am feeling sluggish and lethargic, I get active so that my heart speeds up just enough to develop a bead of sweat for about 30 minutes. But about fifteen minutes into the activity I am already feeling renewed and ready for action. Adrenalin can be fun, but the effect of endorphins decreases anxiety and increases creativity.

Even mild forms of exercise have been proven to elevate mood. But wait, there is more. Studies have also shown that people who exercise regularly have a greater resistance to viruses and infections and even cancer.

Remember, getting fit does not need to be painful. Do not exercise to the point where you cannot carry on a conversation, but you do want to sweat.

Discovery 2. Juice for taste and water for thirst

Brad started to drink six large glasses of juice a day, believing that it was good for him. He needed to lose weight, and having tried various diets devised by others, he decided to try one of his own: less beer and more juice. He knew that beer packed the calories on, but was unaware that juice also gave him more calories. He did not realize, moreover, that juice cheats the body of exercise. The juicing machine does the work that your body was designed to do. Drinking juice is almost the same as drinking liquid sugar. Brad could not figure out why, after one month of drinking juice several times a day, he had put weight on rather than lost it.

Finally, a friend who had taken a course in nutrition explained the problem and gave Brad some good advice: Drink juice for taste, but take water for thirst. Brad immediately cut his juice intake down to one small glass at breakfast and stuck with water for the rest of the day. Within a month the scales showed a difference. Brad was amazed how a slight tweaking of his lifestyle affected his weight.

One of the oldest stories to address the importance of nutrition is from the Bible. Hundreds of years before the time of Christ, there was a man named Elijah. He led the unofficial opposition to the king and queen who had absolute power over their realm. One day, the queen had had enough of Elijah's irritating rise in popularity and threatened to kill him. Elijah had just run a marathon distance from a mountain and was sleeping by the gate of the city, trying to recover and prepare for the next showdown with the throne. He was tired, hungry and expended; he was burned out. When he received the queen's message, he panicked and ran for 40 days into the wilderness where he prayed a suicidal prayer: "God, let me die!" In his depressed state, he believed he was alone in opposition to the evil rulers.

The story goes that God sent an angel to him, not to heal him or to strike him dead, but simply to bring food and water. Once Elijah was in a better state of mind, having eaten, God pointed out to him that he was not the only one left; there were 4,000 others in the opposition movement and Elijah should retrace his steps, confront the threat and lead the movement. His story is a good lesson that a proper balance between nutrition, exercise and rest is vital to maintain a healthy emotional and mental state.

Discovery 3. Sync the beat

My father was raised on a farm. Even after he moved to the city, married and started a family, he called his brothers regularly, asking how the seeding was going, or whether they had gathered in the harvest before the first frost. I never appreciated his sensitivity to the seasons until we moved to Japan. Our house overlooks a cluster of rice paddies. Behind us there are only houses. Except perhaps for the weather, you could never tell, by looking at the houses, which season it is. The rice paddies, however, pass through a cycle of transformations throughout the year. Each year, we watched with amazement the old Japanese women, permanently bent over from years of farming, planting rice by hand below the surface of the brown water that had flooded the paddies. Soon afterwards, small green sprouts would appear through the surface of the water, until there was nothing but bright green carpets of rice stalks. The same ladies would come out a few months later and harvest the rice. We became accustomed to the processes that the fields went through. This experience has helped me better understand my father's appreciation of the relationship between people and the earth. Rhythm is good.

This may seem at odds with the theme of this book, which encourages the embracing of change. My point is that life cannot be in a constant of flux. Wherever we are, and whatever we are doing, routine is good, as it gives us a beat to which we synchronize our daily lives. I do not like taking business trips (though I do so because I must). Although I enjoy going to new places and meeting new people, I don't like my daily rhythm being disturbed.

Not everyone is like me, but I have discovered that going to bed early and getting up early is how I operate best. Others operate well with the opposite routine – they are at their best at night and it takes them a while to get up and going in the morning. My wife is one of these people. She marvels that I can get up at 5 am or even earlier; and by the time I have taken the 30 steps to my writing hut at the back of our house, I am able to sit at the keyboard and start writing and answering emails. I accomplish more in those two hours before breakfast than I can in five hours afterwards. But the most important thing is that it works for me, and therefore I have come to jealously protect those early mornings. Sometimes I have to stay up later, but I still tend to get up early. Find out what beat your body wants to dance to, and organize your day within that groove.

Brad: a case study

I have already introduced Brad to you. Let me tell you a bit more about him. He is a father of two energetic boys, is over six feet tall and until a few months ago weighed in at 250 pounds. Brad was quite happy with life until his boys got to the age when they wanted to wrestle. Brad's soul was willing but his heart was unable to keep up. His gasping and groaning usually cut the play sessions short. He was out of shape and his sons paid the price.

Brad decided to seek the help of a friend who was a personal coach. At first the weekly discussions focused on goal-setting. Brad listed twelve things he wanted to achieve, most of which were noble but hard to measure: be a better dad, treat the neighbours better, be a nice person. But three of them were measurable and the coach encouraged Brad to focus on those: buy a house by Christmas, lose 50 pounds by the following summer, and compete in a triathlon. The coach suggested that if Brad paid attention to the measurable goals, the immeasurable ones would take care of themselves.

At the next session, the coach asked Brad to identify any impediments or lifestyle habits that were deal-breakers. After some discussion it became clear that Brad's daily rhythm needed to change. Typically, Brad surfed the TV or Internet late at night, eventually falling asleep with the remote control or mouse in his hand. When his bladder woke him and forced him to the bathroom, Brad would crawl into bed for the last four to five hours of sleep. He would usually sleep past the first alarm in the morning and eventually leap out of bed, wash, get dressed quickly and run out the door, shouting goodbye to the family and grabbing a cappuccino on his way to work. His daily routine was destructive.

For two months, the coach centred on lifestyle changes; diet was never discussed. Emphasis was placed on less TV and Internet and more reading, and on going to bed earlier and getting up earlier. Within weeks, Brad was in a calmer state of mind; he was more relaxed and, at first weigh-in, discovered he had actually lost a few pounds. Nutrition, exercise and eating lifestyles were then addressed. Within nine months, all of his goals were realized: he had purchased his first house; he had lost 50 pounds in weight; and he had signed on to his first triathlon.

Brad's story is not that unusual, but it is inspiring. How did he do it? Here are a few lessons we can learn from Brad's success:

1. Progress was incremental. Brad had goals, but he had to take several necessary steps over a period of time to achieve them. The first was simply to go to bed earlier and get up earlier, and to read more. In the 1980s, business gurus flocked to Japan to learn from the success of Japanese manufacturers. What they discovered is that the Japanese believe in the *kaizan* concept: small, qualitative improvements over a period of time lead to greater efficiency and a better product. *Kaizan* worked for Brad. His immediate rewards were a drop in stress levels and a dramatic increase in energy levels. This motivated him to keep going.
2. Brad became informed. Like me, he discovered that water should be drunk for thirst, and juice for taste. He knew he was becoming overweight and decided voluntarily to lay off the beer. He had been doing this for months, but with no real change in his weight. His coach pointed out that he was simply replacing the beer with juice, having large glasses of juice with each meal as well as in between. He had to learn that what seemed like good sense was actually harmful. Brad then set himself on a quest to find out what he should eat and when.
3. Brad became accountable. A weekly phone call from his coach helped keep Brad motivated to do what he said he was going to do. It was the dreaded thought of having to tell his coach that he had not succeeded that kept him sticking to his weekly goals.

NTL is neither a diet book nor a "how-to-get-fit" volume. But it is intended to inspire you to live a healthy life.

Executive summary

Fitness is fundamental to ensuring a super-sized future. What you invest in your health today brings immediate and long-term rewards. That is not to say that you have to be super-fit, but:

1. If you are sweating, you are winning.
2. What you put in determines what you get out. You are what you eat and drink.
3. You should develop and maintain a rhythm of daily life that suits you.

Action plan

1. Look back over the past month and assess how many times you exerted yourself to the point of breaking a sweat. Ideally, you should try to "sweat" at least once every two days.
2. Take stairs rather than elevators whenever possible.
3. Seek sound nutritional advice from your doctor.
4. Weigh and measure yourself. Then set a goal. But do not measure or weigh yourself again for several weeks.
5. Focus on lifestyle changes and not fad diets.
6. Set yourself incremental goals ... remember, the gradual approach works.
7. Sign up for a race, even a five-kilometre walk. It will help focus your training.

Dialogue box

What are my key health and fitness goals?

1.

2.

3.

What are the deal-breakers that will prevent me from achieving them?

1.

2.

3.

What steps can I take?

1.

2.

3.

Caution box

Seek professional advice. Do not embark on a fitness regime before receiving input from a medical professional. Ideally, you should talk to someone who practises sports medicine, but if this is not possible then see your general practitioner.

The beach

Jud surprised himself. He was never one for beach holidays, but this one had been great. On previous holidays, he had found himself exhausted after a short swim or an attempt at volleyball. Gasping for breath and feeling prickly from the heat, he would retire to a beach chair, order an ice cream and fall asleep under the shade of a nearby palm. Jud would usually return home plumper than when he arrived. "But not this time," he determined.

Jud found he had stamina and could snorkel for hours. He even joined in a two-hour volleyball match with some students who were taking a couple of days off college in Davao. He found himself setting out on early morning runs, jogging along the bending paths of the rainforest surrounding his cottage. It had been a wonderful two days, but now Jud was ready to go. He was looking forward to having dinner with Roberto and his mother, and then going on to the next leg of his trip.

He had one more stop in Oceania before flying on to Los Angeles. He missed Kathryn terribly and ached to be reunited. But in spite of his loneliness, he knew he owed it to himself and his father to see this journey through. He knew that the changes taking place within him were more than just physical ... his soul was being reformed.

7. Curves

"If you find a path with no obstacles, it probably does not lead anywhere."

Harriet Beecher Stowe, 19th century novelist

"There's not one thing – except the loss of my daughter; no, not even the loss of my daughter – for which I would rather not have been present. I'm happy that I was there for the military coup, that I was present in the terror that came afterward, that I lived in exile, and that I was present when my daughter was sick and when she died. Nobody had to tell me about it, I was there. I would not like to have missed any of the pain or the losses because I like interesting times very much, and I hope that the rest of my life will be interesting, too. I don't want a happy, comfortable life. "

Isabel Allende, 20th century novelist

Leaving Davao for down under

The evening spent with Roberto and his mother left Jud enriched but exhausted. What was expected to be a walk down memory lane brought a few surprises. Jud had not fully realized the extent of the pain that his mother had endured before her death. Roberto told him that he would often sit by her hospital bed through the night, holding her hand and talking to distract her from the pain.

"She never gave up hope," Roberto said. "She was a woman of faith and she felt she would be healed." He paused. "Your father was strengthened by her strong conviction. He reeled with shock when the doctor told him she only had hours to live."

Jud remembered clearly: it was the night he had lost his faith. Now, sitting 8,000 miles away, recalling the death of his mother, the anger, confusion and sadness surged to the surface. "How could it be?" he cried out suddenly. "Where is God when such a good woman can die at such an early age?" He turned to look out the window in an attempt to hide the tears that were about to stream.

Roberto did not answer the question, but after a moment, began to talk of Jud's father and how his life had changed after the death of Jud's mother. Jud needed no reminders. He had watched his father give up his salaried position, not because he was depressed but because he needed time to mourn and reorient his life. A phone call from his dad had unsettled Jud. It was short and to the point, and did not invite discussion or argument; it was more of an announcement: "Jud, I have decided to quit my job and diversify my life. I know you will have lots of questions, but I do not want to discuss them over the phone. I am happy for you to come and see me and we can talk face to face, but believe me, this is something I must do. I know some may call it a midlife crisis, but with your mother gone, I have decided to redirect my life. I have dreams that I have suppressed for years, and consequently I have a growing inventory of regrets. I intend to rectify that. There are things I need to do, and people I want to see; I want to make some of my dreams come true." When the call finished, Jud fretted about his dad's welfare: it was as if he was the parent, and his dad was the wayward son. Jud did not mind so much that his father had quit his job; he just found it a little worrying, not to say embarrassing, to have a father who was unemployed and drifting.

Roberto told Jud stories of his father and showed him some of the letters he had received from him in the months after Jud's mother died. They were the words of a man with an inquiring mind, searching for something more.

Roberto asked Jud where he was heading next.

"I don't know, actually," he said, "but let's find out." Jud opened Envelope 7. Inside was a postcard displaying a sketch of a river meandering in giant S-turns to the horizon. There was also another smaller sealed envelope bearing instructions not to read the contents until Jud reached his next destination. Jud read the postcard out loud:

> *Dear Jud,*
> *Roberto is a treasure to me. I trust you have found him the same. I have more to say, but not until you arrive at your next destination, which is New Zealand.*
> *It is a land of surprise and opportunity.*
> *Dad*

Tip 7: Straight-line lives are boring

A few weeks ago, not far from my home, thousands of naked men paraded through the streets to celebrate, in spectacular fashion, their manliness. It is an annual gathering for men who have recently turned 40 years old. Fittingly, it takes place near a shrine erected in honour of the penis. Timed to take place just before the month when Japanese companies offer promotions to their workers, the festival serves as a pep rally for 40-plus men, who fear that this could be their year of calamity. The Japanese call it *Yakudoshi: yaku* means "calamity" and *doshi* means "year". It is a year that men dread. Here's why.

Japan is famous for its "salarymen": men in suits, hired directly out of university, who stay with their company for life. Entire generations of men enter companies and advance through the ranks, receiving new assignments and increases in salary each April. By the time they reach the age of 40, the possibility of mass advancement has ended and only the chosen few move into the rarefied air of senior management. There are not enough places to go around. All their lives, men pursue the dream – being one of the select few – but most are relegated to uninspiring tasks. *Yakudoshi* is the year when the salarymen get burned. For 20 years, lured by the prospect of being one of the chosen, they work hard, never leaving the office before the boss and ingratiating themselves to the right people by achieving good results for the company. But when they enter their forties, they face the moment of truth: was it all for nothing? Indeed, for most, it is *Yakudoshi*: rather than moving up, they are moved sideways, and for the rest of their working lives they are mere worker bees. The only reward is job security.

For women, *Yakudoshi* happens about eight years earlier. In Japan, the workplace is dominated by men, and the home is the domain of women. It is fine for a woman to have a career in her twenties, but if by age 32 a woman is not married and in charge of a household, she may never be, and will thereby miss out on what the culture says is the best role for her.

Although Japan is sociologically different, many men and women in other parts of the world suffer their own form of *Yakudoshi*. It usually comes in the form of the soul-searching question: "Is this it?"

I spoke with a man in his thirties at a dinner party. He spoke confidently of his future plans. He had his life planned out, right up to the age of retirement. Another person standing in the circle said, with a twinkle in his eye: "Well, you know, the best-laid plans ... !" He did not complete the sentence, for the point had been made: life has its unexpected turns.

Kosuke Koyama, a Japanese theologian, is author of *The 3 Mile an Hour God* and *Water Buffalo Theology*. He writes: "The womb is not a cube." He points out that man makes right angles, but God makes curves. Right angles and straight lines are efficient, but boring. God's world of curves, bends and mysteries makes life interesting. Koyama argues that God never intended life to be a straight line, but to be a journey with unexpected twists and turns. In short, life's surprises remind us that we are alive.

The womb is not a static shape: it is flexible, adapting to the changes of the emerging life being nourished within it. When a life enters the womb only to eventually leave it, we are shown a principle that life is really an ongoing series of entering and leaving, entering and leaving. Each entry stage is preparation for another leaving stage.

Straight-line lives are rigid and unnatural, and become humdrum. It often takes a shock to liberate us from such a life.

One way to avoid straight-line lives is to diversify our interests. An older person once gave me some wise advice: "Have many dreams, pursue them all, and just make sure that at least one of them pays the rent." This is contrary to the notion that to succeed, you must only have one focus, one goal, and doggedly pursue it until you achieve it.

Sometimes, for a season, a single focus is necessary, but overall, fulfilment can only be found in diversity. One of the smartest decisions I ever made was to give up my straight-line life, put my wife first, follow her to Japan, and re-invent myself. I decided to diversify and find ways to wake up each morning and be able to choose what to focus on that day.

Japan is a difficult place in which to lead a diverse life. In Japan, people like to pigeonhole you, and the tool they use is the business card. I have to carry six different business cards – I have one for HOPE International, one for my company, three for various boards I am on, and one for Adventures With Purpose. While there is the odd time when I struggle to determine which business card to use, I delight in preventing people from pigeonholing me.

Diversity protects us from a distorted perspective. If I am consumed by one activity I can easily be buffeted by storms within that small world, but when we have a number of universes to call home, we find that the view within each one is different; being able to switch views means we remain on an even keel. This does not mean we say good-bye to passion. The opposite is true. In all that we do, we should give our all – but not 24/7 .

Proponents of the belief that success requires 150 percent commitment and many sacrifices have a dim view of those who lead a diverse life. "They are not committed," we are told. Workers who are considered to lack commitment are subject to pep talks and, at times, punishment. But this is a not-so-subtle form of manipulation employed by straight-line people who want to form you into their mould. I contend, as no doubt you have gathered, that it is unnatural to lead a straight-line life and that it is never too late to do something about it.

Metanoia is part of the vocabulary of theologians and management consultants. Theologians know it as the Greek word for "repentance", which means "turning". Management consultants talk of turning your company in a new strategic direction. Both usages are appropriate: turning is part of life. Sometimes it is failure or even catastrophe that forces us to turn, and other times, it is simply our choice to turn from something good to something better. Sometimes the turns are slow and almost imperceptible, like the turning of our bodies from youth to old age. Other times, the change is sudden and unexpected: losing a job, the death of a loved one, divorce, or other circumstances that befall us.

The memory is vivid of my father being flung from his seat in a high-speed turn. We were moving house to a new home on a hill. My father had rented a moving van, the type where the seat is perched high. You literally had to climb up into it. The accelerator, brake and clutch pedals were on top of long pegs that extended a half-metre above the floorboards. I was in the back, on the floor, looking up at the back of my dad's head, seeing only the sky beyond. The road leading up to our new home had a couple of S-turns and my father entered the first far too fast for a vehicle with a high centre of gravity. The van leaned heavily to the side, sending my father sliding off his seat. He struggled to keep his hands on the steering wheel while standing on the floor beside it. Then he struggled to climb back up on to the seat. It was a funny sight. Life often throws us a curve while we are turning at high speed, and we are thrown off-balance as a result. In hindsight, we can laugh about it, but at the time, danger was very much present. Whether life's curves are gradual, or by choice, or thrown at us unexpectedly, they remind us that we are alive. And it is never too late to use those challenges as a catalyst to bring about positive change in our lives.

Executive summary

Life has many surprises: some good, some bad. Each experience has the potential to enrich our character.

1. Life is not always predictable.
2. Straight-line lives are boring.
3. "The womb is not a cube!"
4. At times, life throws us unexpected and unwelcome curve balls and we are forced to turn and change directions: even these unpleasant times can turn us towards a new direction.

Action plan

1. List the parts of your life that you would describe as straight-line. How could you bring variety and diversity into your life right now?
2. Is your social network simply an extension of your personal tastes and experience? In other words, are your friends all like you? If so, look for opportunities to add to your social repertoire by involving yourself in new activities.
3. How do you view your failures and hard times? Make a list of what good has come as a result of them.

Dialogue box

Key forces that keep my life going in a straight line:

1.

2.

3.

What failures or twists of fate have befallen me in the past?

1.

2.

3.

What lessons have I learned?

1.

2.

3.

Caution box

The management of change requires patience and wise counsel. Whether you are having change thrust upon you or you have instigated it yourself, seek advice from wise counsellors as you make decisions.

Tremors in New Zealand

The flight from Manila was uneventful. It was Jud's first visit to New Zealand. On the plane, he watched a documentary about the country's emerging film industry fuelled by Peter Jackson's Lord of the Rings. *The "can do" spirit seemed to be a national trait.*

Jud stepped out of the terminal and shuddered as the cold autumn Auckland air touched his skin. He wasn't sure where to go and what to do. The envelope he held in his hand had a message written on the outside: "Do not open until you have arrived in New Zealand." Uncertain whether he had to catch a second plane or go into town, Jud retreated back into the terminal and ordered a cup of coffee. Once settled into a private corner of the arrival hall, he opened the envelope.

Dear son,

Welcome to New Zealand! I have a surprise for you. But first, take a look at the picture of the river on the postcard you read while you were in Davao.

Life is like that river: always moving forward but not in predictable fashion. If you look closely you will notice the river snaking across a flat plateau. There is no reason for the giant S-turns. The land is flat! Why doesn't the river take the straightest route to the horizon? Surely it takes more energy to turn than to go straight. You would think that the momentum of the water coming from behind would force the river to go directly to the horizon, but it chooses to twist and turn. Are you getting it?

Life has its unexpected turns, and you are going to experience one now. On the back of this message you will find a phone number. It is for a man named Grant who is seven years older than you.

He is your half-brother.

Your mother was married before. She had a whirlwind teenage romance that resulted in a pregnancy. The young man married her, but he began to beat her. Fearing for the life of her child, she ran away and filed for divorce. Her parents put pressure on her to put the baby up for adoption. She

struggled for weeks, and finally agreed that it was the best thing to do for the baby. Five years later, I married your mother, and two years after that, you were born. On the night I asked your mother to marry me, she told me of her previous marriage and the existence of Grant. Later, when you came along, we decided, rightly or wrongly, not to tell you. Our reason was to protect the privacy of Grant. He was adopted by a couple who, we learned later, much later, had emigrated to New Zealand to start a vineyard on the South Island.

About ten years ago, Grant decided to search for his birth mother and found her, a few weeks before she died. Many tears were shed, and questions asked and answered. Your mother made me promise that I would find the right moment to tell you. She had wanted to tell you herself, but was afraid of how you might react and did not want to spoil her final time with you. She was torn. She loved you so much.

Grant returned for the funeral and I had hoped for an opportunity to introduce the two of you, but you were so caught up in your grief that he and I both felt it was bad timing. Then several years went by, and each year I wanted to take you to New Zealand to meet him. Sadly, you are now here on your own.

I wrote to Grant and said that you might be coming. I hope you are not too angry.

Love, Dad

Jud was stunned; the turbulent thoughts and emotions triggered by his father's note almost overcame him. It was all he could do not to explode. He felt it had been a mistake to read the note here. He needed a private place. Almost in a state of shock, he walked outside, jumped into a cab and said, "Take me to a hotel, any hotel; just get me there as fast as you can."

"Airport hotel or downtown hotel?" the taxi driver asked.

"Downtown," said Jud, without knowing how far it was. "Not too expensive, but somewhere with a view."

"I know just the place," the taxi driver said.

Normally, Jud would have sought out the local hostel, as he had come to enjoy the company of fellow travellers. But he needed space, a place to deal with the news that had come out of the blue.

In the hotel room Jud threw his bag on the floor, the letter on the night stand, and himself face first on the bed. His emotions were caught somewhere between anger and a deep, penetrating sadness. So many thoughts raced through his mind ... he did not know how to deal with them all. After a few moments, he rolled off the bed and stood at the window, staring blankly at the harbour directly in front. He saw the ferries coming and going to the fingers of land on the other side of the bay and to the islands beyond the mouth of the harbour. He struggled with the implications involved in making a phone call to this so-called half-brother. He could not believe that through all those years, his father and mother had maintained the lie.

Jud, the man, cried like a little boy denied the bike he had always wanted but never knew why he couldn't have. "I've been robbed," he sobbed, hammering the chair with his fist. Hours later, he felt numb and strangely alone. If only his wife were here.

By late afternoon, Jud found the courage to make the call. A sturdy, heavily accented male voice answered.

"Hello. Is Grant there?" Jud asked.

"Speaking." It was a short, almost abrupt answer. Jud got the impression that Grant was at his desk working and when the phone rang he had answered it while still shuffling papers.

"My name is Jud; I believe you know my father?"

There was a brief pause and an almost imperceptible but evident intake of breath. "Sure do, mate. I'm Grant, of whom your father spoke. Been 'spectin' your call."

"Uh, yes," Jud stammered, groping for polite words. "I'm staying at a hotel next to the ferry terminal at the harbour. Could we get together?"

"Yeeeus," Grant drawled, in a typical Kiwi accent: "How about I meet you outside the ferry terminal at a café called Chin Chin in about an hour?"

"Sounds good," Jud lied. "I'll be waiting out front."

Jud was there early. His flight had arrived in the morning, and it was now late afternoon. He needed caffeine. He saw Grant coming and knew immediately that this was his mother's son – the same blue-green eyes as his mother. The kinship was unmistakable.

Jud rose and greeted Grant with a stiff handshake. "Can we walk?" he asked, knowing this was rude, but he did not want to sit across a table with Grant, not just yet at least.

"Of course," Grant replied.

Walking was good, Jud thought. This man was a stranger, and walking was a convenient way of avoiding intimate eye contact. Jud was not ready for familial intimacy. The two men strolled up the hill towards Metro City, and then left to Albert Park. The paths were steep and Jud noticed that Grant was struggling for breath. Jud wasn't sure why he quickened the pace. Grant didn't complain and sped up too.

They looped through the park, back down onto Victoria Street. They were mostly talking about New Zealand and the vineyard owned by Grant's family on the South Island. Grant was in charge of sales and marketing; that was why he lived in Auckland, a city that one out of three Kiwis call home. Jud noticed the Albert Park Backpackers' Hostel, sandwiched between two stores called The Beat Merchants and The Hemp Store. They eventually ended up at the top of the Sky Tower where they sat down for the first time, with a cold drink, each admiring the view through the window.

Jud yelped when suddenly a body dropped from the roof overhead. He stood up and watched the body fall to the ground below. Grant laughed and slapped Jud on the back.

"It's OK, mate. It's very safe. Anyone can do it – anyone, that is, prepared to cough up a couple hundred dollars."

Jud sat back, relieved that he had not just witnessed a suicide, and laughed too.

"C'mon, bro," said Grant. "Let's go get something to eat."

8. Service

"Love your neighbour as yourself."

Jesus Christ

"It is one of the most beautiful compensations of life that no man can sincerely try to help another without helping himself."

Ralph Waldo Emerson, 19th century American, poet and philosopher

"Happiness cannot come from without. It must come from within. It is not what we see and touch or that which others do for us which makes us happy; it is that which we think and feel and do, first for the other fellow and then for ourselves."

Helen Keller, an inspirational role model to millions

Reflections over the South Pacific

Jud spent a week in Auckland. He and Grant got together most days for a meal or a drink in the evening. Jud spent his days exploring, walking and thinking. On the Saturday they went sailing with a group of Grant's mates. The day started in glorious sunshine, but as they circumnavigated Waiheke Island, they hit some bad weather and anchored in a bay for the duration of the storm. In the evening, in calm seas, they sailed back to Auckland harbour.

Grant was easy-going and did not push Jud to talk on any other terms than that of a new acquaintance. Jud took note that Grant's friends admired and respected him. During the course of the day on the boat, he had heard anecdotes of the various times Grant had helped them out of sticky situations. Grant seemed embarrassed. "C'mon, guys. Jud will think I've set you up."

That night in a bar in the harbour, when Jud and Grant were alone, Grant asked, "Where you off to next?"

"I don't know," admitted Jud, "other than that on the outside of the envelope marked 8 it says, 'Fly to Los Angeles and read the letter inside this envelope once you are on the plane.'"

"When do you leave?" Grant asked.

"Tomorrow," Jud replied.

Grant took Jud to the airport the next day to see him off. The two men had developed a sense of friendship bordering on kinship, and they promised to stay in touch.

Jud was so tired he immediately fell asleep, missing the meal and the first movie. He woke somewhere over the mid-Pacific. After a stretch and a stroll to the rest room, Jud took out Envelope 8, hoping there were no more surprises.

> **Dear son,**
> **I hope you are not too angry with me. I said in Envelope 1 that this was a journey I had wanted to do with you. I know that the surprise waiting for you in Auckland must have been a shock to the system. I have prayed long and hard that your meeting with Grant would go well for you both. I hope it has. I trust that you will be able to connect again.**

But for now you need to move on to the final phase of this journey. You need some time to reflect on what you have experienced on this journey but you are not quite ready for that. In fact, it could be unhelpful, if not dangerous, to do so right now. Let me explain. It is important to be introspective and self-focused and to have dedicated times of reflection, sorting out your values and your vision. But I have learned that this is best done with an understanding of the wider context. It took me a long time to discover that the best way to help myself was by serving others.

At the airport in Los Angeles there is a surprise waiting for you. You will like this one. It is Kathryn. She has arranged for the two of you to join a work team for a week in Central America somewhere.

Kathryn helped me to concoct this adventure. She loves you very much. At first when I told of her of my idea and asked her to help me, she was reluctant and needed a bit of persuasion, but when she bought into it, she did so big time. You are going to spend a week together doing something for others. The coming week should put your own journey into perspective, but it will also remind you that whatever you do for others, it is you who gets the greatest reward.

Love, Dad

A few hours later, Jud and Kathryn met in the transit lounge of Los Angeles Airport. They held each other for a long time.

"I've missed you more than you can know, and I have so much to tell you," Jud whispered. He broke the embrace, leaned back, looked his wife straight in the eye, and said, "Just how much did you collude with Dad on this whole enterprise?"

"All will be revealed in due course," Kathryn laughed. "But for now we have a plane to catch."

"Where to?" Jud asked.

"Guatemala," she replied. "We're joining a group from my church for a week in a barrio outside Guatemala City. We're going to build a community centre."

Tip 8: Reap the rewards of serving others

The truth is self-evident: in serving others you help yourself. Focusing on other people is a sure antidote for dealing with your own pain. It is a time-tested prescription for those who slip into the abyss of self-pity. Service offers a distraction from ourselves and provides us with a wider context in which to examine our lives: it helps us see the bigger picture. Service is a handy tool for those wanting a change and looking for ways in which they can be challenged. There are plenty of opportunities, as near as your local town, and as far as Timbuktu.

I will leave it to you to find out about the various ways in which you can serve others locally. But I also highly recommend travel and service, as it allows you to experience a new culture and serve others within a different socio-economic environment. Travel is a way of broadening your education and enriching your life, but travel need not simply be a self-indulgent exercise: we can do something for others at the same time. And this form of travel is increasing in popularity. Why? Because people end up discovering as much about themselves as they do about the places and people they visit.

Exploration has always been at the heart of adventure travel, but with most of the earth's surface mapped and analyzed, there is a new kind of exploration – that of the heart. Each year, more and more people are opting out of package holidays to embark instead on adventures that involve joining a cause and learning more about themselves and the world in which they live. This alternative form of adventure travel is tough, dirty and sometimes dangerous, but brings a heap of satisfaction to those who take the risk. Opportunities abound for those with a restless spirit, a big heart and a healthy dose of "dare 'n' do". These types of adventures fall into three categories:

1. Sponsored challenges

Whether it is a long-distance bike ride, making your first bungee jump, or kayaking around remote islands, it is easy to convert your adventure into a fundraiser for worthy projects and people. Many charities organize their own events and recruit people to join them. Typically, you pay all of your expenses and are required to raise an agreed amount of money for the non-profit organization. Such an event has a lasting effect as it not only stretches your belief in yourself and what you can do, but also, through your own fundraising efforts, raises awareness about the world's poor and shows how you can help others. Many people are attracted to the physical challenge of an endurance event, while at the same time being intimidated by the fundraising aspect. However, once they complete the challenge, most say it was the fundraising that was the most rewarding.

I was twelve years old when I had my first "adventure with purpose". I and 10,000 others walked 35 miles around our hometown of Winnipeg, Canada; it was a sponsored walk in aid of the poor in Haiti. I cannot recall what specifically prompted me to do it, but it was probably the challenge of doing something I had not done before. My first adventure with a purpose was not to be my last. After the challenge was successfully completed, I felt a great satisfaction in not only finishing the walk but also in raising several hundred dollars. I learned that an adventure with purpose is much more satisfying than self-indulgent play. My eyes were opened that day: I not only realized that I was physically capable of a gruelling walk, but the world's poor came into my universe. As an adolescent, my life's course was set by that challenge.

Check out the possibilities on the Internet where you can find a myriad of destinations and a variety of sports; trekking and cycling seem to be the most popular but you will also find challenges that involve cross-country skiing, kayaking, sailing and much more. You can also go to

www.hopeglobalchallenge.com and www.adventureswith
purpose.com for a variety of opportunities to raise money
for the poor.

An adventure with purpose accomplishes two things: it
changes you while it assists others.

2. Work teams
Does building something with a team, while living with
locals for a few days or weeks, interest you? There are many
organizations that offer working holidays. My two
favourites are HOPE International Development Agency
and Habitat for Humanity. While HOPE and Habitat both
entail building things, other charities involve environmen-
tal research, archaeological digs, and even restoring old
stone walls in rural England. Don't be under any illusions
though. The primary reason to go on a work team is not to
change the world, but to experience a personal transformation. Let's face it: labour could be hired locally, at less
expense. Work teams, though, help people develop an
understanding of global issues by forging mutual understanding between cultures. To find out more, contact a
local charity or talk to someone who has been on such a
project.

HOPE International offers a program for people of all
ages called UNION: an acronym for Understanding Needs
In Other Nations. Like other organizations, HOPE have
been taking teams to other countries for many years and
have developed a good program where participants do not
merely hop on a plane and go, but are taken through a cur-
riculum of study that focuses on issues facing the poor –
and the rich for that matter. For more information go to
www.hope-international.com.

3. Fact-finding trips
A fact-finding trip can involve a sponsored challenge, a
work team, or can be a stand-alone project. Many organiza-

tions offer trips (at your own expense) to visit projects in the developing world in order to see first hand the plight of the poor and the good that credible, sustainable projects can bring. The benefit of going on a trip like this is that everything is organized for you; great care is taken to avoid voyeurism and patronizing photo opportunities. Usually these trips are short and designed for folks who are busy but have the money to take a few days off to make a flying visit to some remote corner of the globe.

Whatever form of adventure travel we choose, we must avoid patronizing the poor. Relief and development voyeurism that imposes our good intentions on the vulnerable, for the sake of self-satisfaction, is wrong. But there are ways to travel with integrity, enabling us to experience other cultures properly. The great thing about any of these options, or creating your own adventure with purpose, is that it serves as a catalyst for change in your life. The education received by the experience, as well as the emotional high that comes with facing a challenge, stays with you, and becomes a significant marker on your journey to personal transformation. One more thing: adventure travel is not just for the young. It is never too late to build a bead of sweat, get your hands dirty and serve others.

Executive summary

Adventures with purpose are more rewarding than self-indulgent play.

1. It is possible to elevate life's adventures with the aim of serving others while helping yourself.
2. There are different types of short-term opportunities to have an adventure with purpose:
   - sponsored challenges
   - work teams
   - fact-finding trips

Action plan

1. Investigate opportunities for adventures with purpose.
2. Next time someone asks you for sponsorship, say yes, and be generous.
3. Don't just go yourself; take your family.

Dialogue box

What have I done recently for others?

1.

2.

3.

What did I learn from the experience?

1.

2.

3.

What kind of adventures would I like to go on with the aim of serving others?

1.

2.

3.

Guatemalan nights

Jud got on with the members of Kathryn's church, which came as a surprise. He noted that contrary to his expectations, they were interesting and easy to work with. What he enjoyed the most, apart from being with his wife again, was working alongside the local bricklayers. As an economist, he was intrigued by their lives, their jobs and the pressures that prevailed within their society. One thing was for sure: these people did not need North Americans to come and do the work of building the community centre. There was a lot of laughter on the building site, usually at the church team's expense: problems were often caused by the clumsy Spanish of the visitors. Once, the site went into an uproar when a wall built by three of the team, without the help of local experts, fell over.

Kathryn was often on the opposite side of the work site, while Jud mixed concrete and did the grunt work for the bricklayers. He spent a lot of time pondering the plight of the poor. Images of Mindanao were still fresh in his mind, as was his recollection that the subsistence farmers he had met there did not seem to perceive him as being better off, but only from a different place. The problems of poverty, sustainable development, AIDS, water-related disease, globalization and conflict resolution were complex, and

Jud had not spent any real time considering them, except when he had written papers at university.

One day, in the midst of loading sand into the mixer, something dawned on Jud, causing a brief shudder: he had cocooned himself in a false and unreal blanket of personal comfort. Even though he was a trained economist, he had no clue as to what economic hardships the majority of the world's people face every day. Jud pledged that he would seek a better understanding, and become involved somehow. The answers would not come easily, but he was being changed through the process of reflecting on them. One thing he knew: while he could not change the world, he could enlarge his own world by forming friendships with people living in different circumstances.

On the final night, Jud and Kathryn talked late. She was eager to hear all his stories of the past weeks. And Jud wanted to hear hers. About 2 am, aware of the thin-walled hotel where they and the team were staying, Jud and Kathryn made love in playful, whispered passion. As they lay in each other's arms in the afterglow, enjoying the stillness, they heard the distant rumblings of Guatemala's lively resident volcano, Pacaya.

The next day on the flight back to Los Angeles, Kathryn leaned her head on Jud's shoulder and fell asleep. Jud stared at Envelope 9, which he had placed on his lap. He felt apprehensive, not wanting his days with Kathryn to come to an end and not knowing where his dad was going to take him next. Careful not to wake Kathryn, he slowly tore the envelope open.

9. Soulcraft

"What good will it be for a man if he gains the whole world yet forfeits his soul?"

Jesus Christ

"The heart of a man is like deep water."

Old Testament songwriter

"It is well to lay fallow for a while."

Martin Farquhar Tupper, 19th century British poet, reformer and early supporter of the volunteer movement

Northern pilgrimage

Dear son,

Your next stop is where you spent four years of your life: the University of British Columbia. Remember how we danced in the living room the day you got your acceptance letter into UBC? We were as surprised as you. But it was your excitement of getting into your university of choice that infected us as we swirled, jigged and yelped through the house. We lived in the glow of it for months. The thrill was repeated when you made it into the London School of Economics for your higher degree. You were so full of optimism and your life was falling neatly into place. After university we watched with pride as you went from one success to the next.

But, Jud, we also watched you grow a bit fatter, your hair thin out, and a strain develop in your relationship with Kathryn. Our worries were confirmed when you came home for Thanksgiving and told us you and Kathryn had agreed to have a short time out from each other. You didn't tell us much, and although you returned to each other a few weeks later, your marriage became a focus of our prayers.

I am sorry for the walk down memory lane. I guess the fact that you are nearing the end of this journey reminds me that I am nearing the end of mine. I am trying to recount all those things that have enriched my life: you are right at the top of the list.

I want you to return to Vancouver, not as a student, but as a pilgrim. Take a few days to reflect on your journey and your life. In particular, ask yourself what your dreams are. Be open to the possibility that the dreams you are pursuing are the wrong dreams. Attend a service or two in one of the chapels on campus, as it will help you focus on things of the spirit. Keep a journal and centre on what is important to you. Now is the time to make some decisions, come to conclusions and search for spiritual insight. I know you are not much of a believer, but my prayer is that God would meet you in some unexpected way.

Believe me, the opportunity you have is to be envied. Not

*many people get a chance to take time out, and reflect on
the meaning of their life.*
    Love, Dad

"I'm off to Vancouver," Jud said.

Kathryn smiled.

"Of course, you know that already. I keep forgetting that
you're Dad's collaborator."

On arriving in Los Angeles, Jud booked his flight to
Vancouver. As he and Kathryn had a couple of hours before their
respective flights, they found a Starbucks and celebrated their
week together by indulging in a shared Frappuccino. Then they
strolled hand in hand through the departure lounge and to
Kathryn's gate. Jud hugged her as he said goodbye. "I love you,"
he whispered.

"I know. I love you too. It won't be long now until you're home."

Tip 9: Touch the sacred ... learn the art of soul survival

"Wells take water out; dams put water in!" declared Clark
as we stood in the Burkina Faso backcountry.

I was visiting West Africa where the Lungren brothers,
Clark and his brother Rob, sons of Canadian missionaries,
were fulfilling their dream of arresting the desertification
of the country in which they were raised. Their plan was
simple: build dams to harvest the bountiful rain that fell by
the bucketload during the rainy season but then simply ran
off, taking precious topsoil with it. Through their efforts,
after two decades, the Nazinga Project has become a flour-
ishing game reserve. This successful project was based on
the simple notion of restoring the water table. The spiritual
application is obvious. To fight the desertification of our
soul, we must focus on restoring the spiritual water table of
our lives. The following insights can help us on our way.

1. Sabbath is an antidote to "burn-out"

The term "burn-out" is well known in our modern culture. I was burned out by the time I turned 40. I spent my thirties seizing every opportunity that came my way, believing that life would pass me by if I stopped. Then one day, sickness brought me to a halt and I realized that I was replaceable! The office where I worked kept going; the committees I was on kept meeting. Life went on – I was not indispensable after all. It was a rude awakening.

When I began researching this book, I wrote to a number of trusted individuals for ideas. One of them, an ordained minister I have known since childhood, wrote back with brutal honesty. I have his permission to include our exchange in this chapter.

Lowell,

1. Everything I want to do requires money. I can't afford to dream or live large.
2. I am married to a follower, who is nauseatingly content to sit on a log and drink her coffee.
3. I am a dreamer whose dreams have died.
4. I have reached for the brass ring, seen it up close but fallen short, afraid to reach again.
5. I am becoming a bitter old man.
6. Life has taught me I can trust no one, including myself.
7. I am in constant conflict. The last thing I want or wanted to be was a minister. I have become that which I dreaded.
8. I do not know who I am.
9. I am lost, without hope for me, my family, the world.
10. Most days I do not want to live any more.
11. I am bored.
12. Life is meaningless, a cruel joke.
13. I do not believe in God or Love; these beliefs have failed me.
14. I am trapped. If I was to truly follow my heart I would be considered by those in my world as a dead-beat dad, a failure, lazy, a freak.

15. I see no use in life or living.
16. I have regrets too numerous to mention.
17. I have made stupid choices, leaving me indecisive and afraid that the choices I am making now are poor ones.
18. I try but cannot seem to reach contentedness or inner peace. I have a troubled mind and equally troubled heart. I have a deep sense of doom and foreboding.
19. I am angry at my way of releasing my anger.
20. I had a map. It was the wrong one.

Will your book help this man?
Your friend

I was deeply concerned by what he wrote and replied immediately:

My friend, your message scares me.
I look at your life and see so much that is positive ... sure, you have been dealt some tough blows, but you have two wonderful children and a spectacular wife, who may be content to sit on the log, but also is exceedingly supportive of you.
Your life is in your hands. People who have lots of money are no happier.
So you have made some wrong decisions. Then change them. Have the courage to step out and change direction.
Sorry, I don't mean to sermonize, but you are an impressive man, one I seek to emulate – I just don't know what to say.
I value you and I cannot fathom what grief I would endure if I were to lose you.
Lowell

To this he replied:

Thanks, Lowell,
The truth is I am bored and burnt out. I am tired of life on the treadmill, living month to month, trying to keep up or play catch-up all the time. All the positives you mentioned

are true and yet I feel so despondent and, what's worse, I see no way out. I feel overwhelmed, am afraid of growing old. If I can barely manage financially now, what will it be like when I am 70? Will I have to work and struggle forever? And so I think of dying, but, don't worry, not by suicide. I couldn't bear to think what that would do to my family. But I think of death as a welcome relief. If I was told I had six months to live I would be delighted! Let's get it over with. I'm tired, Lowell. Tired, bored, depressed. I'll get through it. Your honest response has helped me in this moment. Thanks. The book sounds great. Go for it.

Your friend

To arrest the deterioration of the soul, a time out is needed. Initially, it may just be a rest: a mindless, lie-on-the-beach, soak-up-the-sun kind of rest. But that will not be sufficient to restore the soul. A sabbatical is needed when attention is given to one's spirit. Burn-out should not be feared, however, for it can put us in a frame of mind where we rightly reflect on our dreams, on what is important to us. Like any crisis, it has its dangers, but also the opportunities abound to explore and restore our souls. In desperation, the nerve endings of our soul become exposed. It is in our desperation that we realize we need something more, something higher, something spiritual to guide our lives.

Every human being needs a sense of purpose or calling. No doubt you have heard the story of the monk who was desperate to know God. After many lonely days and cold nights in the mountain-top monastery, the young novice went to an older monk and asked in desperation: "How can I know God?"

"Do you really want to know him?" the older man asked.

"Yes!" replied the monk emphatically.

"Then follow me," instructed the older man.

They walked down the mountain, across the plateau, and down the steep hills to the valley floor, where they found a stream. The older monk led the younger man to a spot where the water was still and deep and told the young man to kneel and get his face close to the water. He knelt, bewildered but expectant.

"Closer," the superior commanded him.

The young monk touched his nose to the surface of the water. Suddenly and violently, the mentor took both hands and thrust the head of the young man under the water, holding him there for ten seconds. To the terrified young monk it seemed he was without breath for ten minutes.

When the old man finally released his grip, the victim shot upright, gasping for breath. "Why did you do that?" he shouted, sputtering angrily.

"You will know God," said the older, wiser monk, "only when you pant for him the same way you pant for breath." The story captures the passion of the Psalmist who said: "As the deer pants for streams of water so my soul pants for you, O God."

2. For faith to grow, mystery must be embraced

My first book, written with the help of Catherine Butcher, a British writer, is called *Never Ending Adventure*. The title, borrowed from John Wesley, the founder of the Methodist Church, describes the essence of faith: it is dynamic, not static. Faith is not a case of clinging onto a few propositional truths: it is always on the move, reaching, probing and searching for more. Bono, the lead singer of the group U2, sang, "I still haven't found what I'm looking for." And a generation agreed.

Shortly before he died, Lesslie Newbigin, who served as a bishop in India for many years, explained that faith was like climbing a rock face. I remember his homily going something like this: "When climbing a mountain the safest position to start your climb is with four secure grips for both hands and feet. But to advance up the rock face of faith, at some point you have to let go, and reach up into the mystery to find something more, something higher to grip."

His metaphor is a good one. We have all been mesmerized by the sight of human "spiders" crawling up a vertical wall without ropes. Sometimes, these climbers let go of two grips at one time in order to move up. Occasionally, a climber is seen dangling from one finger, before he hurls himself up over a ledge to a more secure place. On rare occasions (usually in movies) climbers will do the ultimate: using their four secure grips as a launching pad, they blast off and for a moment seem suspended in space before reaching a new place on the rock face. One thing is for sure: you will never enjoy the thrill of getting to the top unless you let go and reach into that unknown. The lesson for us is that we should not live in fear that our faith is fragile. Faith is designed to be tested, and the truths we discover are to be steps towards a higher place, not the destination itself.

3. God is a jack-in-the-box

God is the god of surprise. He not only meets us while on retreat or in spiritual gatherings but also in the mundane repetition of everyday life. He is like a jack-in-the-box: as we turn the handle of everyday life, God is always there, but occasionally, and without warning, God bursts into open view, revealing grace and mystery, and resulting in a moment of pure joy. The encounter may not be dramatic: it is often subtle, and only in hindsight do we realize that the moment we experienced was spiritual in texture.

Many of us were raised to think that spiritual disciplines relate to attending meetings, praying, and the devoted and daily study of scripture, when in fact the living of our lives is the most spiritual thing we can do and is where we will most likely encounter the divine. God is in the routine. Whether it is a time of joy or deep grief, God will come to us in the most surprising of ways. We must be careful not to miss him.

We ignore our spirits at our peril. Sadly, busyness

results in neglect of the soul, and the result is spiritual starvation. When that happens, the soul gives up; feelings die. Thankfully, it is never too late to correct spiritual deprivation. For those who are burned out, a sabbatical is needed. Others may simply need to cultivate an awareness of mystery and an expectation that at any moment, God, who is always present, may leap towards us and touch us with grace.

Executive summary

Often, CEOs and leaders in different fields complain that there is not enough time to reflect in their lives. This is a problem facing many people on the treadmill of career advancement. We need to create time to reflect and to develop the art of soulcraft.

1. Burn-out can result in either emotional numbness or dangerous introspection. Sabbath is the antidote.
2. Do not be afraid of mystery. Reach into it for answers.
3. Look for God in the mundane.

Action plan

1. Plan into your schedule times to write a journal, reflect and meditate.
2. Read a book that evokes profound thoughts.
3. Go to church, one that will allow you to ponder great themes. Avoid the churches that only seek to rope you into lots of work or programs.
4. Actively look for those moments when the jack-in-the - box God surprises you in the routine of everyday life.
5. Incorporate physical exercise into your spiritual disciplines. Endorphins are God's gift to us. We were designed that way.

6. Don't simply take a beach holiday; it will not be life-changing. Use it to have rest, but then move on to a real sabbatical.

Dialogue box

How would I describe my spiritual state?

1.

2.

3.

What prevents me from becoming spiritually stronger?

1.

2.

3.

When have I experienced God as a jack-in-the-box?

1.

2.

3.

Wanderings and ponderings in Vancouver

Jud booked into the youth hostel near Jericho Beach from where he could reach the University of British Columbia in less than an hour's walk. For many days he enjoyed visiting the old haunts where he and his friends used to hang out. He strolled through the corridors of the buildings where he had attended classes. Each day, as his father instructed, he took part in a chapel service, and whiled away hours in the library. He found one particularly meaningful book in the Regent College Library called The Cloister Walk *by Kathleen Norris, the story of a poet who had spent time in a Benedictine monastery. It reminded Jud of the writings of*

Thomas Merton, which he had read many years earlier, in a less busy time of his life. Reading of Norris's account of her life while in the monastery helped Jud make the mental transition from being a traveller to being a pilgrim. Usually, he would leave the library and walk for hours, pondering what he had read and thinking about his life in general. He usually found that about 45 minutes into a long walk his mind would gain an amazing clarity.

One afternoon, his thoughts focused on his father and Jud decided to write him a letter. No sooner had the pen touched the paper than the tears began to flow. He penned the pent-up words he had wanted to get out of his system ever since the revelation down under, that he had a half-brother.

> Dad,
>
> I have two things to say.
>
> First, I forgive you. I do not understand why you made the decisions you did, but deep in my soul, I trust you and therefore I forgive you.
>
> Another thing, Dad: THANK YOU! You have not only given me life, but you have saved my life. The trip has changed me ...I realize that the values on which I base decisions need review and that I need greater balance in my life. I have you to thank for that. I love you.
>
> Jud

10. Time

"Nothing comes from doing nothing."
William Shakespeare, 16th century playwright

"TV is chewing gum for the eyes."
Frank Lloyd Wright, 20th century architect

An old dream revisited

He sat on the sand, eyes closed, his back resting against a log that was smooth and flat except for the gnarled knot pressing into his lower back. Jud relished the fading warmth of the sun on his face. As he shifted position, he opened his eyes just in time to see the sun going down in dazzling glory on the distant horizon of Howe Sound. The orchestral sound of the incoming tide was gentle and rhythmic: it was as if the sun was saying goodbye and the tide was saying hello. Soaring seagulls caw-cawed overhead and the fragrance of the west coast rainforest was sweet and pleasing. The street lights of Vancouver's West End flickered in the light of dusk, while the glow of the setting sun cast its spell on the windows of high-rises, standing like tall, thin centurions guarding Stanley Park.

Jud felt nourished, rested and at peace. He was ready for the fray of everyday life again, but not on the same terms as he had before – his values and dreams had been renewed. In the days of his wandering through the campus of the University of British Columbia, exploring the riches of the library and attending the chapel services at Regent College and the Vancouver School of Theology, Jud had embraced dreams that had lain dormant. Some of his dreams, he realized, were misguided and inspired by fanciful, adolescent notions of what adulthood was. New, mature dreams were emerging in their place. Jud was gaining clarity, in sharp contrast to the depressing fog that had shrouded his life prior to the trip.

The light was fading, so Jud took out his notebook, and read a scribbled list of goals he had written during the day: exercise more, eat better, read more vigorous tomes, spend more time with Kathryn and get involved in community service. He placed the notebook back in his rucksack and took out the envelope marked 10. It was creased and crumpled from nearly three months of travel and was larger and heavier than the previous envelopes.

"I sure hope it's a good one," Jud said to himself as he weighed the envelope in his hand, thinking of how long he had *lugged it around the world. He gently peeled back the lip, tugged on the letter inside and began to read.*

> *Dear son,*
>
> > *Your journey is nearing its end. But before you take your final flight, I have a challenge for you. The challenge I have set for you is timely, for it is a lesson about the clock. You see, time is ever ticking away, and we can either choose to squander it or invest it. Goals are achieved only as we use the time given to us wisely, investing it in worthwhile pursuits. It is a simple concept but can have a profound impact on a life: an hour can never be relived. Make your life, every minute of it, count.*
> >
> > *Now, about the challenge: you have always wanted to learn to fly. Remember how you went on and on about it? Many nights as I tucked you into bed as a young boy, you would say to me, "Dad, one day I'm going to be a pilot and fly an airplane all by myself."*
> >
> > *"I bet you will, Jud," I would reply.*
> >
> > *Years later, I smiled when you wrote to me from university saying that you were taking weekend flying lessons at a flight school. But then a few months later, you quit. In your letter to me, you told me that flying was harder than you thought and you felt overwhelmed.*
> >
> > *This is the challenge: go back to that flight school, and finish what you set out to do. It is a matter of applying yourself and putting in the time. You may not have enough time to put in the necessary hours to get your pilot's licence but if you work hard and are diligent, you may just get good enough to have your first solo flight.*
> >
> > *Good luck and happy flying!*
> > *Dad*
>
> *PS When your flight school is nearly over, please phone David Turner, a friend of mine in New York. His number is on the back of this letter. I know you are eager to get home to New Jersey, but I want you to set up an appointment to visit him. He is expecting your call.*

Jud smiled. The book he had lugged around the world was, in fact, his pilot log-book. He opened it and looked at the date of his last flight as a student pilot. Memories he had not recalled for years came flooding back. He remembered barely passing ground school and how he had grown frustrated by not learning as quickly as he wanted. But despite the impatience, and his chronic fear of heights that gnawed at him before each flight, Jud had loved flying. When he walked away from the airport on the day of his last lesson, he let go of his childhood dream.

But sitting on the beach looking at Vancouver, with the log-book in his hand, he could feel a wide, boyish grin coming across his face.

"I could solo?" he asked out loud as if his father was right beside him. He fantasized for a few minutes, imagining it as a reality.

Tip 10: Stop watching TV

Last year, at a business lunch gathering, I interviewed a novelist, Barry Eisler. Barry, a 30-something, is not only a novelist but also a husband, a lawyer, a judo black belt and a connoisseur of fine whiskeys. (I am sure he has plenty more achievements and interests.) During the interview at the sports bar I asked him to share a tip for succeeding in life with the small gathering of entrepreneurs. Without hesitation Barry replied, "Stop watching TV." At the heart of Barry's argument is the belief that humans have an innate desire to "start and finish" tasks and that TV deceives people into believing that they have accomplished something.

His admonishment and argument make sense. Compare watching TV an hour a day for three months with spending an hour a day studying a second language for the same period of time. At the end of an hour of language study students often feel frustrated and discouraged. They feel as if they have accomplished nothing. On the other hand, if you watch a TV program from beginning to end there is a subtle, even imperceptible, satisfaction that you have completed something, evidenced by the absence of frustration and discouragement. But in both cases, the opposite has taken place. For if you watched TV an hour a day for 90 days, you would have accomplished little other than a numb brain and a flattened bottom. However, if you studied a second language for one hour a day over 90 days, you would have an extended vocabulary, improved pronunciation and a deeper grasp of grammar than you did before.

Of course, TV is not all bad. In right measure it can be a handy tool to relax at the end of the day, keep informed of important news or enhance your education. But for many, TV has become an addiction. And, worst of all, such people sit with eyes glued on the flickering images, while feeling more and more resigned that what they see on the screen will be the closest they get to realizing their dreams. TV becomes a dream substitute. But it only takes a small decision to stand up, turn the blessed thing off and devote the 30 minutes to something more active and constructive! Not only will you have prevented your metabolism from slowing down, but you could be a half-hour further down the road to making a dream come true.

My friend learned 2,000 *kanji* (there are several thousand *kanji*, or characters, in the Japanese language) in six months. He found the right method, stuck with the plan, stopped watching TV and accomplished his goal. When he told me of his success, I was intrigued. I have lived in Japan for seven years and have only mastered a pitiful 100 *kanji*. I decided to try his method. I surprised myself. Through diligent effort a few hours every day for two months, using his method, which also happened to be fun and interesting, I gobbled up several hundred *kanji*. The method happened to work, but my point is that I was inspired by his accomplishment.

Success breeds success. At first, the successes will be small, but enjoying many small successes gives rise to confidence to tackle bigger challenges. This is common sense, but it is amazing to see how many people fail to embrace it as a lifestyle. To succeed you have to allocate time to tasks, in order to accomplish your goals. This notion brings us back to the first tip – Get a map – where we noted that having a vision in itself does not mean that it will be realized. Nor does being realistic in measuring how far we are from that goal. What will make our dreams come true is the diligent giving of ourselves to the steps required to get us from where we are to where we want to be. Every step we take towards our goal requires time and effort. But in the end, through steady, incremental advancement, we will achieve our goal.

Many people fail to rise to the challenge of acquiring a new skill or setting out on a new course because they feel they have to drop everything else to accomplish their goal. Indeed, some people have the talent for singular focus over a long period of time. We have been taught to admire people who doggedly pursue their goal at the sacrifice of everything else. But I suggest that this is a wrong model, and even a dangerous one. Humans are complex beings who have a diversity of skills and needs. To focus on career at the expense of family, for example, is wrong. We are beginning to realize that. But I also contend that simply to have a dual focus, where family and career are in equal tension, is also harmful and unfulfilling. It is possible to remain energized and productive in the workplace and in the home, while pursuing other dreams as well. While it is undeniable that people can become overstretched, most people only stretch themselves in one direction. But the whole of our being, body, soul and mind, needs stretching, and why not reach for several dreams at the same time? Of course, some may require more effort and a greater allocation of time than others, but the more diverse your life is, the more balanced and whole you are likely to be as a person.

My advice to you is: Have many dreams and pursue them all, but make sure at least one of them pays the bills.

Executive summary

Human beings have an innate need to "start and finish" things.

1. The best way to advance is incrementally.
2. It only takes fifteen minutes a day dedicated to exercise, learning a language, or acquiring a new skill to see progress. At the end of each hour you may be discouraged, but if you are diligent over three months, there will be measurable outcomes that will boost your confidence.
3. Time is ticking; start now to work towards your goal. The time of completion may be a long way off, but if you don't start, the time when you would have completed the task will one day arrive, and you will stand there, empty-handed, with nothing to show. For those who have the courage to face the reality of having squandered their time, the sensation is horrible, but it also compels us not to let it be repeated.

Action plan

1. List some practical goals: aspirations you often muttered to yourself, and others you would like to achieve. Be honest. No matter how silly they seem, put them down.
2. Now write beside each goal what is stopping you from achieving it. I suspect that for some of them at least, you will write two words: TIME and MONEY. I cannot speak for the second, as I do not know your financial circumstances, but I do know that every human being has the same amount of time in the day.
3. Now do a time assessment of your day. Once again, be honest. Are you making the most of your time? Do you channel surf, play video games, sit dozily in the pub or in an easy chair at home?

4. Choose a goal and work out a plan as to how you are going to achieve it.
5. In a few weeks or months, you can achieve the goal. When you do, you will be motivated to go for something bigger.

Dialogue box

What takes up most of my time?

1.

2.

3.

What dreams do I have that I believe are unrealizable?

1.

2.

3.

What steps do I have to take to make one of those dreams come true?

1.

2.

3.

Caution box

Do not be ruled by time. Some people successfully carve up their day into fifteen-minute segments. Admire them, but unless you are certain you are one of the few who enjoys life that way, don't aspire to be like them. Have space in your schedule to allow for the spontaneous and the unexpected opportunity.

Flying high over the Fraser Valley

Jud was elated. He was actually in a plane by himself, a thousand feet above ground. The week had been hard work, particularly the first two days in ground school. Although Jud had been through it all before, the instructor insisted on an intense crash course to review the myriad issues involved in flying: weather, the mechanics, airspace protocol and air safety. Fortunately, Jud had renewed his student pilot licence a couple of times since attending UBC, perhaps due to an unconscious choice to keep his dream alive.

During the course of the week he spent about 20 hours in the air. On the seventh and final lesson he and his instructor flew circuits over the now familiar terrain of Langley City, then moved up the Fraser River and practised landing at a couple of grass airstrips. Having landed back at Langley Airport, Jud taxied the Cessna 172 back towards the hangar, adjacent to the flight school. Terry, the instructor, opened his door, hopped out quickly and said, "OK, Jud, take it up yourself for one circuit."

"Me? Alone?" Jud's eyes went wide!

"Yep, you're ready for it; just remember all I've taught you and you'll be fine."

After Terry closed the door, and gave the thumbs up that he was safely clear of the aircraft, Jud taxied out to the runway. The control tower gave him clearance for take-off. Jud pushed the throttle in, adjusted the flaps, gained speed, and slowly and gen-

tly pulled up the nose of the aircraft and began to climb. After a few hundred metres, he banked and banked again so that the airport was to his left. Looking down, he could see the small images of cars, planes and people on the ground. His face almost hurt from the big grin that had spread across it.

"I'm flying. I'm really flying." Jud scanned the horizon all around him and then dipped the wings a couple of times. "I'm in charge of the aircraft and I'm in the sky by myself!" he revelled.

As he flew over the Newlands Golf and Country Club, he banked again and then turned into his final approach. The landing was not as perfect as he would have liked, but as he taxied towards the hangar where Terry was standing waiting, the air traffic controller's voice came over the speaker: "Congratulations on your first solo flight."

Epilogue

"I get by with a little help from my friends."

John Lennon, songwriter

**"You cannot teach people anything.
You can only help them to discover it within
themselves."**

Galileo Galilei, scientist and thinker

New York, the final frontier ...

Jud had never met Dave Turner, and was surprised when Dave recognized his voice on the phone.

"You must be Jud," Dave said. "You sound like your father. Are you on your way to New York?"

"Yes, I've booked an overnight flight tonight. I arrive in the morning."

"OK. Give me a couple of hours. Your dad asked if he could borrow some technology which I need to organize. Can you phone me back? Everything should be set up in an hour or two, and I can let you know what time to come by. OK?"

"Sure," Jud agreed.

"Your dad was a good man, a great man, and I'm looking forward to meeting you," Dave said.

"Thanks, me too," Jud replied.

An office seemed an unlikely location to end his three-month journey. Jud was curious. One thing he knew: not to underestimate his father's ability to engineer a surprise. He had no idea what to expect, nor did he try to speculate. When Jud phoned back, Dave asked him if 1 pm was alright.

"Yep, I can do that," Jud said. He wrote down Dave's address and thanked him for going to so much trouble.

"No problem, Jud. Anything for your dad."

Jud tried to sleep on the "red-eye" flight to New York but he felt apprehensive. The next bed he would sleep in would be his own and then the real challenge would begin: would he slip back into the routine that had become his life, or would he have the inner fortitude to follow through on the goals he had written in his journal? Flying solo had boosted his confidence that anything was possible. But he feared that once back in familiar surroundings, "muscle memory" would kick in and he would revert to living his life on autopilot. His train of thought was broken by the thud of the plane's landing gear hitting the tarmac.

Once in the terminal, Jud spotted Kathryn.

"Congratulations on your solo flight," she whispered in his ear as they hugged.

"Thanks," he replied. "I've missed you. Let's get out of here."
They walked outside to hail a taxi, their arms tightly around each other's waists.

In the taxi, Kathryn was full of news and stories: nothing of a dramatic nature, but simple, everyday kind of news. Jud felt nourished by his wife's energy. He had so much to tell her, but there was too much, far too much for the moment, so he settled for simply describing his time leading up to his solo flight and how great he had felt when the air traffic controller congratulated him over the radio. He showed Kathryn the solo certificate and the photo of himself beaming alongside Terry, his flight instructor.

They had a couple of hours to kill before the 1 pm meeting so they strolled through Central Park. It was a fine spring day.

"So what is this 1 pm meeting about?" Kathryn asked.

"No idea," Jud said. "All I know is that Dad asked his friend Dave for some technical help. We'll know soon."

Border crossings are exciting but stressful. It is more than just the necessity of being processed; it is the fear of the unknown that lies beyond. Whether it is Cambodia, Canada, Croatia, Cuba (I have crossed all those borders more than once), passing from one territory to another can be tense, but the lure of the unknown draws us forward. It is natural to sense fear when we are about to do something new. But faith in the future will pull us through.

Sometimes we may feel that faith longs to propel us to new heights but fear holds us back. There may have been times when, no matter how much you wanted to go forward and believed you should, fear fought to prevent you like an eagle that is tethered to the ground. But faith and fear need not be opposing forces. To feel fear is natural, and should cause us to step back, question and double-check that what we are doing is good, and reasonable. In some ways, in order for faith to be exercised, there needs to be an element of fear or a sense of danger.

You could say that fear forms the threshold of faith. But fear must not be relegated to a hoop that we must jump through to achieve our goal. When we are about to do something new, the sense of risk, the fear of danger, causes our senses to be awakened and we become very alert. It is only a transitional phase, but a phase we should not rush through too quickly, for while we are in this state we become more spiritually aware.

In an earlier chapter, I spoke of how love compels us to greater levels of curiosity, compassion and celebration. It is in times of nervousness that we are able to experience these dimensions of life in bountiful measure. Yes, I am scared, but I am too curious to stop moving forward. To discover the riches of new experiences and different places is too important to me and to the ones I care about. The prospect of adventure propels me forward, but fear increases my awareness. The more familiar people become with their surroundings, their routine and their life, the greater they grow deaf, blind and oblivious to nuance and subtle shifts in ambience. Treasure after treasure goes unnoticed. But when change and its companion, nervousness, are present, what was monochrome becomes spectacularly diverse and intriguing. When it comes to personal re-invention, the fear is felt most acutely at the moment when you have to let go. The planning and preparation may have been gradual but there still comes a key moment when you have to release your grip on what is familiar and comfortable. And the moment after is much better than the moment before.

Fear alerts us that there is risk

Fear urges us to proceed with caution. Only an idiot jumps from a bridge on a bungee cord bought at a DIY store. Have you ever abseiled, or repelled? There is nothing more unnatural than standing on the edge of a cliff and walking over it – backwards at that! It takes a lot of courage: one has to put trust in ropes, techniques and the person holding the safety line. The first time I did it, I looked into the eyes of the instructor and the assistant who were holding the safety rope, searching for assurance that all was OK. I was looking for the love! Could these people be trusted? Did they care about me? The fear I experienced was acute. Once I took the step, committing myself to a new set of rules, I was positively enthused. I was doing something that I thought impossible – and it was exhilarating.

Change involves risk. Whether the change is thrust on us, or is the result of our personal initiative, the inherent risk will bring with it some measure of fear: our families, our money and our reputation can all be at risk. Therefore, risk management should be taken very seriously.

So what should the fear of the unknown compel us to do? I suggest we ask ourselves the following questions:

1. Are my choices value-based?
2. Have I put thought and care into planning?
3. To whom am I accountable?

To some measure, other sections of this book deal with the first two points. As we conclude this book together, I want to emphasize the importance of accountability. Accountability and transparency go hand in hand. As you consider possible changes in your life, endeavour to remain transparent with selected friends and family. But I suggest that beyond them, you find a mentor or two who can guide you through the process of change.

Personal life coaches are becoming popular. While some are put off by the thought of employing these, others have found it works. My friend, who owns a successful communications company, has four personal coaches: a nutrition coach, a spiritual coach, a strategic planning coach and a physical trainer. It works for him. Whether it is a trusted mentor or a paid professional, a coach can help you change your life's course or reach a specific goal in a number of ways:

1. Information. A coach usually has more experience or knowledge in a given subject than you do. He or she is not just a listening ear but usually someone who has "been there, done that". Think of your coach as a mentor, one who gives tips, advice and personal assessment with the view of helping you improve.

2. Accountability. In addition to giving advice, a coach holds you accountable to your goals and plans. A good coach will not only help you determine your goals and strategy, but will expect you to adhere to them. A coach may not be as interested in your dream so much as in the road map that you use to realize your dream. That weekly phone call or meeting will help you focus and remain disciplined in achieving what you set out to do.

3. Inspiration. A coach celebrates your achievements and helps you in your recovery from failure. A good coach helps you learn from your failures, move on, and be better off for the failure. A coach also helps you realize that each success is not an end in itself but a step towards the next goal and achievement. He or she puts your failures and successes into perspective.

It is never too late to embark on a new adventure. Life is made full by the fun and adventure of embracing your dreams! NTL kicked off with the enigmatic Benjamin Franklin. I shall close with the words of another famous American, Mark Twain:

> Twenty years from now you will be more disappointed by the things that you didn't do than by the ones you did do. So

throw off the bowlines. Sail away from the safe harbour. Catch the trade winds in your sails. Explore. Dream. Discover.

Friends in New York

Jud arrived at the unfamiliar address ten minutes ahead of time. He had asked Kathryn to come up with him, but she had declined.

"I'll be at Starbucks around the corner," his wife had responded. "Give me a call on my cell phone when you're about to leave. We'll eat out before we take the ferry back to New Jersey. OK? There's not a lot of food in the apartment."

"Sure," Jud had said. "I've no idea how long I'll be or what's going to happen, but I'll see you when I see you."

Jud took the elevator to the 43rd floor and followed signs to Ryco Digital Group. He introduced himself to the receptionist, who immediately recognized his name and made a phone call. Three minutes later, the elevator door opened and a tall man in a dark suit walked out.

"Hi, Jud," the man said with a million dollar smile. "My name is Dave Turner. I knew your dad very well, and when he asked me for a favour I was more than happy to help out. Follow me; the video conference room is ready."

Dave led Jud through the open-plan offices. The deep plush carpet gave way under his feet with each step, and Jud noted how energized, yet peaceful, the office atmosphere was. They walked past an expansive corner office; Jud noticed Dave's name on the door and the title "President" underneath. The video conference room was next door to Dave's office. Jud only had a moment to enjoy the view, as no sooner were they in the room than Dave pressed a button, and blinds silently covered the windows, leaving the room dark except for the glow emitted from a large screen at the end of the room.

"Please sit down, Jud. All will be revealed in a few moments," David said, offering Jud a chair facing the screen.

Suddenly a video image of Jud's father appeared on the screen. He was in his bed at the hospital. With a voice that only hinted at the strength it once had, he said, "Jud, you are now at the end of the journey you have taken at my bequest. No more envelopes, and no more surprises. I have a final word of advice for you. It is almost certain that I will die soon; the cancer that took your mother has come for me too. But you know, I am dying a happy man, and I have you to thank. Jud, you once declared you did not want to be like me. You told me of the pledge that you and your friends made in London many years ago, and that you were going to hold each other accountable for the pursuit of your dreams. It troubled me at the time but I respected you for it and it got me thinking about my own life.

"When your mother died, I was awakened. Up to that point in my life I had believed that my career was paramount, but your mother's death made me realize that life itself was most important and that it should be lived with a curiosity and celebration, and a disposition towards service. So I reoriented my life. I decided to leave the company and start the consultancy, as you know. But I also got involved in a variety of other activities, including a non-profit organization that I founded, and in addition I took up painting, cycling and travel. The consultancy paid the bills, and I began to enjoy my work life a lot more, when it became only one of many things I was involved in.

"I was lucky to meet three people who inspired me with the notion that a diverse and balanced life is possible and healthy. One of the three is David, who is sitting in this room with you. He kindly organized this meeting. The other two are Ted in Beijing and Judith in London. These three people have taught me a lot. I won't bore you with the details as to how I met each of them, except to say that I have known them for about ten years. I have observed them succeeding in their respective spheres at work and learned from them when they have failed. They are not single-focus people. They each have a variety of interests and are all active in community service and outreach of some sort. They have agreed today to hear the story of your journey. They may even

share some of their own experiences. I wanted you to meet them and them to meet you. They are among my dearest friends and most trusted mentors. I am not suggesting they need to become yours, but I wanted you to meet the people to whom I am indebted for showing me a way to live life to the full.

"So, thanks to the wonders of modern technology, David's generosity, and Ted's and Judith's willingness to get up at an unearthly hour, you are going to enjoy each other's company for the next two hours. I trust that telling them of your journey and the lessons you have learned will help clarify and solidify your reawakened dreams and goals.

"So I guess this is goodbye. Be assured that I am dying a happy man. I love you, Jud."

Jud fought back tears as his father's image faded out. The images of Judith and Ted came in. He felt embarrassed, but the sight of Judith dabbing the corner of her eyes with a tissue, and Ted looking straight into the camera with eyes wide open but a hint of a tear welling up, put him at ease.

"Hello, Jud," they chorused together.

"Your dad was a special man who did a special thing for you, Jud. We're curious to hear about your adventure." Judith said.

"We are all ears!" Ted leaned back in his chair and smiled.

Postscript

Jud had been home six months and was settled. His round-the-world adventure had begun to blur in some of its detail, but Jud was aware that he had changed. The video conference in New York was significant. Judith, Ted and David had not only listened to the story of his trip, but had probed him with searching questions about his dreams, values and spirituality. Jud found the session liberating. They all asked him to keep in touch. After the video conference, Dave invited Jud into his office.

"Your father said he learned from us," David said. "But in truth we were mentored by him."

Jud and Dave talked for a few more minutes. As they rose they shook hands. As Dave gripped Jud's hand, he looked at him squarely and said, "Don't waste the last three months. Use it as a springboard from which to make qualitative life choices. You can be assured that we are watching with interest, and will stay in touch. You can see us as your informal advisory board. Call any time."

With their help, and the full support and participation of Kathryn, Jud returned home to a new life. It had familiar touchstones, but now there was a sense of adventure with which he woke up most mornings. He felt alive.

It was 6 am Saturday. Jud had one email to write and two longhand letters. The email was to Robert and Sarah, whom he had contacted within hours of getting home several months ago. He had phoned each of them, describing what had happened on the trip. He had also promised them he would report to them how he was doing with the goals he had set.

> *Hey, Robert and Sarah,*
>
> *Trust you're both well. It's been a few months since we last chatted and when I promised to let you know how things were going. Well, to be frank, I was happy when the trip ended. Seeing the world is great but it's true that "there's no place like home". And home is even better now! Things I had grown familiar with are so much more interesting. It's as if my antennae have been raised. I'm noticing people, smells and activities that I haven't noticed before. I*

could go on, but I promised you an update on some decisions I have been considering. Well, here they are:

1. *First of all, Kathryn and I have decided to wait no longer: we're going to have a child. Due in five months. We're both excited! After the adventure that my father laid out for me, I realized how important it is to pass a family's history and wisdom on to the new generation. I want to leave a legacy to someone too. I regret that it took me this long to agree to something Kathryn has always wanted, but I guess, better late than never.*

2. *I am not going to pursue flying. I did what I dreamed of doing: flying an airplane by myself. But in accomplishing my dream, I'm satisfied.*

3. *I have decided to stay on with my company for two more years, and then move on. Perhaps I'll become a consultant – or Kathryn and I are even musing about starting up our own business.*

4. *I've kept up my physical fitness regime but am now running about ten kilometres every other day. Kathryn, who was always fitter than I, has persuaded me to sign up for a half-marathon in three months. I'm kind of enjoying the training, but I'm a bit nervous about actually running in a competition.*

5. *Finally, I guess it is relevant, that we are now helping to raise money for an NGO that is doing work in the Philippines promoting organic farming and sustainable development. The need is so great, but I came home convinced that each person had to do his or her part. Roberto, the Filipino friend I told you about, put me onto them, and I'm pleased to say that we're staying in contact.*

6. *I have also got involved in a micro-finance project in Africa. I'll be working with the US office, which focuses on funding strategies and building the fund that is available to the rural poor who need access to inexpensive capital, lent on compassionate terms to help them get a leg-up out of their debilitating poverty. I am buzzed by the potential. It seems a good fit with my*

training as an economist and my newfound vision to be a giver and not just a taker. No doubt you will hear more about this.

7. As you know, I'm not much of a churchgoer, but I am now going to Kathryn's church most Sundays. I find the setting-aside of an hour a week for reflection and meditation enriching.

8. Finally, we have decided to invite my brother Grant to come and spend next summer with us. I'm not sure how he will respond, but I hope he decides to come.

That's it for now. How about you guys? Whassup with you? How is the new product line, Robert? Have you opened the Taipei office yet? How about the extension on your practice, Sarah... is it finished yet? I look forward to hearing from you.
    Jud

Jud hit "Send", turned away from the computer and put his pen to paper.

Dear Grant,
    I have fond memories of our time together in New Zealand. I'm sorry if I appeared distant, but I'm still getting used to the idea of having a brother. The more I think about it, and reflect on the days that you and I spent together, the more I feel excited about the prospect of getting to know you more. How about coming to visit us for a few weeks next summer (your winter)? If it helps, we can even set up some appointments with potential distributors for your wines.
    I do hope you can come. And I look forward to hearing from you.
    Your brother, Jud

Jud leaned back in his chair for a moment and looked out the window. The dawn chorus was celebrating a new day, and the smell of freshly cut grass accented the beautiful autumn morning. In a few moments, he would be out on his training run; he was already looking forward to it. But there was one final letter to write. He pulled out a drawer and removed a postcard he had purchased in Tanzania. He gazed at the picture of Mt Kilimanjaro for a moment, recalling his climb, and then turned it over and began to write.

Dad,

Thank you. I miss you, but I know you have left something of yourself in me. I have good news: you and Mom are going to be grandparents. I am sorry that this didn't happen sooner, as I know that you would have been great at it.

Dad, you will never know how grateful I am that in the midst of your own suffering you were thinking of me. The adventure you gave me taught me many lessons for how to live a large and full life. Be assured that I am not going to squander your investment in me. I will live my life as a tribute to you.

I love you.
Jud

Acknowledgements

I am indebted to the following people who assisted me in some form during this project: Faith Bateman, Jordan Bateman, Matt Hughes, Jeff Kucharski, Scott Moore, Lorna Olson, Annie Pickersgill, Kirstie Sobue, Brent Sheppard and Andrew Westland.

I owe particular thanks to Greta Sheppard, a fellow writer, my mother and a creative collaborator; and to Tony Collins for his belief in this project and for the support of all the staff at Lion Hudson.

Finally, I am profoundly grateful to Kande, my wife, who has been my partner for many an adventure. I can't imagine my life without her.